THE USBORNE BOOK OF
BRITAIN

Contents

Maps

THE USBORNE BOOK OF
BRITAIN

Story of the landscape · Gazetteer · Maps
Places to go · Things to see and do

Revised Edition

Jan Williamson and Susan Meredith

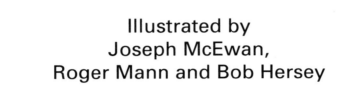

Illustrated by
Joseph McEwan,
Roger Mann and Bob Hersey

Maps by Swanston & Associates

Designed by Graham Round

Revised by Victoria Parker

Additional material by Mary Anne Evans, Robyn Gee and the Area
Managers of Usborne Books at Home.

First published in 1980 by Usborne Publishing Ltd,
83-85 Saffron Hill, London EC1N 8RT
Copyright © 1992, 1980 Usborne Publishing Ltd.

The name of Usborne and the device 🎈 are
Trade Marks of Usborne Publishing Ltd.

Printed in the United Kingdom

The Story of Britain

Millions of years ago the shape of Britain was not at all like it is today. For much of the time Britain's land was under the sea and was not even in the same position on the globe.

This story tells you how Britain's rocks were made and how they rose and sank many times before they changed into the shape Britain is now.

About 4,600–3,800 million years ago

1

Scientists think the Earth started off as a ball of hot, liquid rock. As it cooled down, its surface hardened to a thin crust. The high parts formed blocks of land and the low parts were flooded by violent rainstorms and became seas.

About 3,000–600 million years ago

2

The oldest rocks in Britain are the remains of ancient volcanic islands. Millions of years later, rivers from nearby continents carried sand and mud into the sea over the rest of Britain. As they piled up, the bottom layers were pressed into new rock.

About 500–400 million years ago

3

Two ancient continents began to move together. They squeezed and folded the rocks between them and pushed them up from the sea to become land. There were many earthquakes and volcanoes. Mountains were made in Scotland, Wales and Northern Ireland.

About 2,500–400 million years ago

The first life

Life began in the sea. Simple plants started to grow and then worms, shellfish and bony fish gradually developed. About 400 million years ago the first animals crawled on to land.

The remains of plants and animals which lived millions of years ago are called fossils. You can see them in many sedimentary rocks, especially around the coast.

Different types of rock

Igneous rocks
Rocks made when hot, liquid rock from inside the Earth cools and hardens.

Granite may be white, grey or pink, but is usually speckled. It is hard and glittery.

Basalt is hard, black and heavy. It sometimes cools into six-sided columns.

Sedimentary rocks
Rocks made in layers under the sea from bits of other rock, sand, mud or shells.

Sandstone feels rough and sand rubs off it. You can sometimes see layers in it.

Chalk is soft and makes a white mark if you rub it on something hard.

Fossils

Limestone is grey, white or yellow. Look for layers and fossils.

Metamorphic rocks
Existing rocks which have been changed by being squeezed or heated inside the Earth.

Slate comes from mudstone. It is smooth and dark-grey and has layers which split apart.

Marble is made from limestone. It may be pure white or have swirly bands of colour.

Time chart

Millions of years ago	3000		570	500	435	395	345
What was happening in Britain	First rocks were made in Scotland. Rocks appeared in Wales.		Most of Britain was under sea. Volcanoes in Wales and the Lake District. Mountains were made in Scotland, Wales and Northern Ireland.			Most of Britain was land. Desert climate	Limestone formed in shallow sea. Tropical swamps covered in coal forests.
Geological name of period	Pre-Cambrian		Cambrian	Ordovician	Silurian	Devonian	Carboniferous

Britain's rocks are made

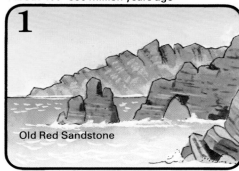

Over millions of years, earth movements have carried Britain across the globe. This journey has caused many changes in Britain's climate and has made a great difference to the rocks that have formed and the plants and animals that have lived.

About 400—350 million years ago

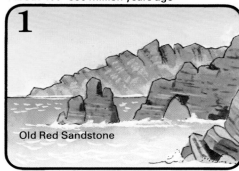

Britain's rocks were south of the Equator and part of a huge continent. The land was desert and a rock called Old Red Sandstone formed. Today you can see Old Red Sandstone in South Wales, Devon and Scotland.

About 350—300 million years ago

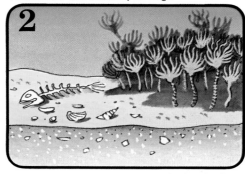

Gradually the south of Britain sank under a warm, shallow sea, which was very clear and full of creatures such as sea lillies. Limestone rock began to form from shells and coral.

About 300—250 million years ago

Britain was on the Equator. The climate was hot and wet, and thick, tropical forests grew on the swampy ground. They were full of spiders, lizards, dragonflies and other creatures.

About 250—200 million years ago

There were new high mountains, mainly in southern Britain. The land was desert again and New Red Sandstone was made. Salt and limestone formed in an inland sea which covered much of northern England.

About 200—150 million years ago

Dinosaurs and flying creatures called pterosaurs first appeared about 200 million years ago. Britain again began to disappear under the sea, leaving only islands of land. Clay rocks and limestones formed in the sea.

About 150—100 million years ago

As the land rose again, the south of England became part of a huge, muddy swamp. Herds of iguanodon dinosaurs grazed in the swamp, feeding on rushes and horsetails. There were many swamps and lagoons.

About 100—50 million years ago

Britain disappeared completely under a huge, shallow sea, which was full of creatures. Thick layers of chalk rock formed from their shells and skeletons. Today you can see chalk on the south coast of England.

About 50—25 million years ago

Mammals spread after the dinosaurs died out (about 65 million years ago). The Atlantic Ocean was opening up to the north west of Britain and the last large area of new rocks was made around London and Hampshire.

280	225	195	140	65	55	38	25
Climate was hot and desert-like, with evaporating lakes and inland seas.		Climate was warm and wet. Most of Britain was under sea, but there were some islands.	Large swamps in southern England. Britain gradually covered by chalk sea.	South-east England was under sea. Atlantic Ocean was forming. Alps began to form in Europe.			
Permian	Triassic	Jurassic	Cretaceous	Paleocene		Eocene	Oligocene

The Story of Britain

Almost all of Britain's rocks have been land for the last 25 million years, but they have changed a great deal during that time to make the landscape we see today.

As soon as new rocks are pushed up from the sea to become land, they start to be worn down again. Wind, water and ice break off small pieces of the rock and carry them away.

In many parts of Britain, rocks on the surface have been completely worn away over the ages to show older rocks underneath and entire mountains have been lowered to plains.

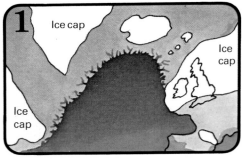

1

About 2½ million years ago the world began to get colder as ice caps spread from the North and South Poles. Several times much of Britain was covered by ice, though in between the ice ages it was often warmer than it is today. At present we may be in a warm period before the next ice age.

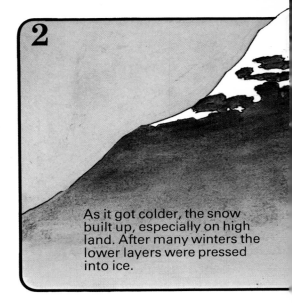

2

As it got colder, the snow built up, especially on high land. After many winters the lower layers were pressed into ice.

4

The mountains of Scotland, Wales and the Lake District were all shaped by ice. Glaciers scooped out deep, steep-sided valleys and hollows. Many of the hollows are now lakes. Ice sheets smoothed and rounded the landscape, but any peaks that stuck through the ice are sharp and jagged.

5

When the glaciers melted, they dropped rocks and mud that they had picked up on their journey. In places these have made a hummocky landscape.

6

Some huge boulders, called "erratics", were carried a long way before being dropped. This one in Yorkshire may have come from Norway.

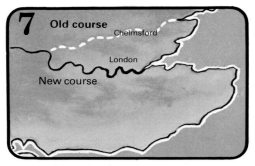

7

Many rivers had to change course during the ice ages. The River Thames used to flow into the sea in East Anglia but as ice sheets moved south, they blocked its route and it was forced to flow east along the front of the ice. After the ice melted the river kept its new course.

Rivers

1

In a wet climate like Britain has now, rivers are important in wearing down rocks. Rivers pick up stones, sand and mud where they are flowing fast in the hills and then drop them on the plains and as they enter the sea. The stones, sand and mud then start forming new rocks in the sea.

2

Soft rock wears away more easily than hard rock, so river valleys usually follow lines of soft rocks, or old cracks and weak places in the rock. Mountains like Snowdon and Ben Nevis are the highest in Britain because they are made of hard rock and so take longer to wear away.

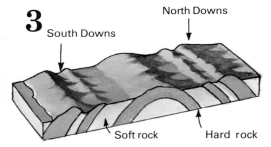

3

The speed at which different rocks wear away makes a pattern of hills and valleys. In eastern and southern England the hard rocks are sandstone, limestone and chalk and they have made hills called "escarpments". The soft clay rock has made broad valleys between the escarpments.

Time chart

Years ago	25,000,000	7,000,000	2,000,000	1,000,000
What was happening in Britain	Atlantic Ocean got wider. South-east England was slowly folded while the Alps were made in Europe.		Some of Britain's youngest rocks were made 2 million years ago in East Anglia. World climate became colder, Ice sheets advanced and retreated across Britain several times. In cold times, mammoths and woolly rhinos lived. In warm times (between ice sheets) elephants and hippos lived.	
Geological name of period	Miocene	Pliocene	Pleistocene	

The ice became glaciers and the weight of more snow falling on top forced them to move downhill along valleys.

3 When many glaciers join together, they make an ice sheet. At one time ice sheets stretched as far south as London.

The glaciers got so big that they filled up their valleys. Then they spilled over to join up with each other, covering all the land between them except the highest peaks.

8 Southern England was never covered by ice, but it had an arctic climate. The soil was permanently frozen and rivers from the ice sheet further north flowed over the surface, cutting valleys in the rocks. You can still see these valleys, although many of them no longer have rivers.

9 At the end of the ice ages Britain was joined to Europe. Then, when the ice melted, it ran into the sea and the sea level rose. Water flooded the Channel and Britain became an island off the coast of Europe. There are old tree stumps around Britain's coast from forests which used to be land.

10 The rising sea drowned the lowest parts of valleys, making many inlets and estuaries. The long inlets in south Wales and south–west England are drowned river valleys called "rias". The deep inlets on the west coast of Scotland, called "fiords", were once filled by glaciers.

Britain now and in the future

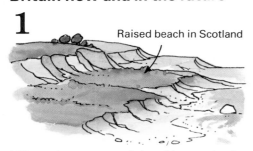

1 Raised beach in Scotland

When the great weight of ice melted from northern Britain at the end of the ice ages, the land slowly rose. Parts of Scotland are still rising today and there are old beaches now far above the seashore. In contrast, the south and east of Britain are slowly sinking.

2 Around the coast waves wear away rocks. Soft rocks often form bays and hard rocks make headlands. In East Anglia the rocks are so soft that about 150,000 square metres of land are washed away every year. The entire town of Dunwich has disappeared over the cliffs in the last 600 years.

3 In 80 million years time scientists think Britain might look like this. New mountains have been pushed up in the Irish Sea and the Channel, so that mainland Britain is joined to Ireland and Europe. There are volcanoes in Ireland, high mountains in south–west England and sea over eastern Britain.

500,000	10,000	8,000	5,000
The first people reached Britain. They were hunters and lived in caves in the Mendip Hills.	The last ice sheets melted in Scotland.	English Channel, Irish Channel and North Sea were drowned by melting ice, making Britain an island.	More groups of people came to Britain from across the sea.
		Holocene	

The Story of Britain

The previous four pages explain how Britain's landscape has been shaped by natural forces over the past 3,000 million years. Here you can see how it has been changed by people over the last 5,000 years.

As the climate began to get warmer at the end of the last ice age, thick forest grew all over Britain. In order to work the land successfully, some of the early farmers started to clear it away. People continued clearing forest for several centuries and now it has almost all disappeared.

3000BC–AD43

1

Celtic village

The first farmers in Britain did not alter the landscape much. They had simple stone tools which were not strong enough to clear much forest and they had to farm the more open hill tops. The Celts had stronger iron tools. They cleared land and farmed small, square fields.

AD43–AD410

2

The first towns and roads in Britain were built by Roman invaders. Many of our towns are on the sites of Roman ones and you can see Roman remains.

AD450–AD1066

3

Viking raid

The Anglo-Saxons ignored the Roman towns and roads and cleared more forest to build villages. They farmed their land in big open fields, divided into strips. The first churches were built, but they were mostly in wood so few have survived. Many present day villages date from Anglo-Saxon times.

AD1066–AD1450

4

Monastery

Town walls

Manor house

By the time the Normans conquered Britain in 1066, some villages had grown into towns, although the population of Britain was still very small. Towns continued to grow during the Middle Ages and you can still see the remains of many castles, churches and monasteries that were built at this time. In spite of the development of towns, most people still lived in villages, farming strips of land for the lord of the manor.

Time chart

Date	3000BC	1900BC	700BC	AD43	AD410
Important people and events	First farmers in Britain arrived from Europe.	More farmers came from the Netherlands and North Germany.	Celts arrived from Europe.	Romans conquered Britain.	Angles, Saxons and Jutes came from North Germany and Denmark. Scots went from Ireland to Scotland. Native Picts died out. Vikings attacked from Scandinavia.
Name of period or people	Stone Age	Bronze Age	Iron Age	Roman	Dark Ages

AD1450–AD1700

5 By 1700 almost all the thick forest in Britain had been cleared away to be used for house building, ship building and fuel.

AD1700–AD1780

6 Gradually the countryside became more like it is today. The big open fields were divided into smaller ones by hedges and ditches. New crops, new machinery and better breeds of cattle were introduced. Farms became more efficient, but many people lost their land and had to move to the towns.

AD1750–AD1830

7 Canals were built to transport heavy goods like coal and iron, and roads improved after the turnpike system of charging tolls was introduced.

Tollhouse

AD1780–AD1900

Slag heap   Pithead

8 Britain became the first heavily industrialized nation in the world. Big towns grew up, especially near the coalfields, which provided power for factories. Railways became the main form of transport. Today you can see disused mills with tall chimneys and rows of workers' terraced houses.

AD1900–Today

9 Towns have got so big that they often join up with one another to form "conurbations". New industries have developed using electricity for power, which means they no longer have to be sited near supplies of coal. Motorways have replaced railways as the main means of transport. Much of the countryside has disappeared and the population of Britain is now about 56 million – nearly 30 times larger than it was a thousand years ago.

AD1066	AD1485	AD1603	AD1714	AD1837	AD1901
Normans conquered Britain. Domesday Book Henry II	Henry VIII Elizabeth I Shakespeare Sir Francis Drake	Charles I Queen Anne Civil War Great Plague and Great Fire of London	George I George II George III George IV Battle of Trafalgar	Queen Victoria Charles Darwin Gladstone Disraeli	World War I World War II Winston Churchill Elizabeth II
Middle Ages	Tudor	Stuart	Georgian Age	Victorian	20th Century

Rock map

This map shows you some of the main types of rock which make up the land of Britain. The key gives you their geological name and you can tell from the time chart on pages 4–6 how many millions of years ago the different rocks were made.

The pictures round the edges of the map show you just a few examples of the types of landscape you can see in Britain today.

Great cracks, or faults, sometimes appear in the landscape as a result of earth movements. This is the Great Glen fault, which cuts right across Scotland.

Edinburgh Castle stands on top of the core of an old volcano. The softer rock surrounding the core was worn away long ago by ice.

Waterfalls are made where a river crosses from hard to soft rock. The soft rock wears away more quickly, making a step in the river bed. This is High Force, one of Britain's highest waterfalls.

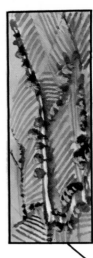

At Malham Cove, in Yorkshire, you can see this strange limestone pavement. It is made by rain water seeping into cracks. The water dissolves the rock and widens the cracks.

Much of the Midlands is pasture land, but in places you can still see ridge and furrow marks under the grass from when the land was ploughed in the Middle Ages.

These ancient hills have flat tops because they have been worn down by rivers. They may once have been as high as Everest.

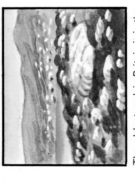

The oldest rock in Britain is in the Western Isles. It is a grey, metamorphic rock, called gneiss. Ancient rock like this lies hidden under newer rocks in other parts of Britain.

The hollow of Red Tarn, on Helvellyn, was once the source of a glacier and filled with ice. The sharp ridge on the left of the picture, which is called Striding Edge, was cut by ice.

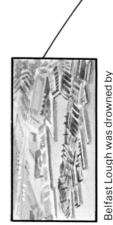

Belfast Lough was drowned by the sea at the end of the last ice age. It is very deep and sheltered, which makes it a good place for shipbuilding.

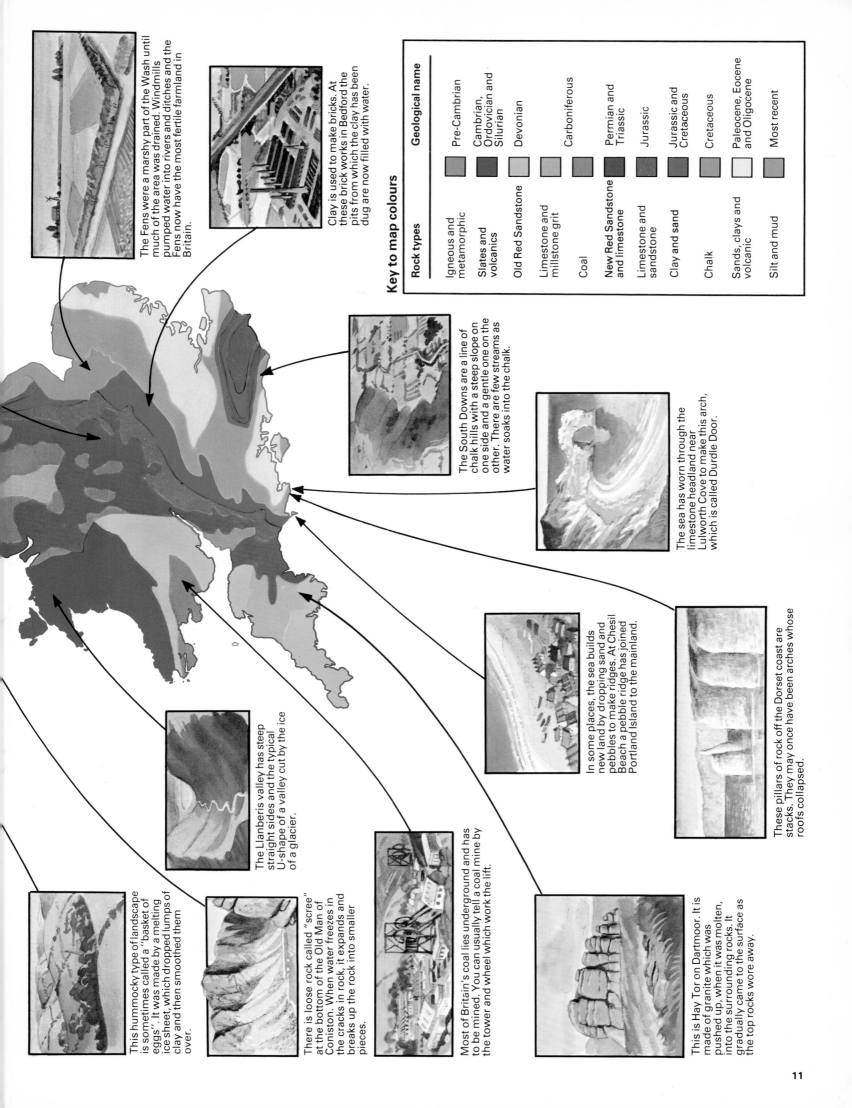

The Fens were a marshy part of the Wash until much of the area was drained. Windmills pumped water into rivers and ditches and the Fens now have the most fertile farmland in Britain.

Clay is used to make bricks. At these brick works in Bedford the pits from which the clay has been dug are now filled with water.

Key to map colours

Rock types		Geological name
Igneous and metamorphic		Pre-Cambrian
Slates and volcanics		Cambrian, Ordovician and Silurian
Old Red Sandstone		Devonian
Limestone and millstone grit		Carboniferous
Coal		
New Red Sandstone and limestone		Permian and Triassic
Limestone and sandstone		Jurassic
Clay and sand		Jurassic and Cretaceous
Chalk		Cretaceous
Sands, clays and volcanic		Paleocene, Eocene and Oligocene
Silt and mud		Most recent

The South Downs are a line of chalk hills with a steep slope on one side and a gentle one on the other. There are few streams as water soaks into the chalk.

The sea has worn through the limestone headland near Lulworth Cove to make this arch, which is called Durdle Door.

In some places, the sea builds new land by dropping sand and pebbles to make ridges. At Chesil Beach a pebble ridge has joined Portland Island to the mainland.

These pillars of rock off the Dorset coast are stacks. They may once have been arches whose roofs collapsed.

The Llanberis valley has steep straight sides and the typical U-shape of a valley cut by the ice of a glacier.

This hummocky type of landscape is sometimes called a "basket of eggs". It was made by a melting ice sheet, which dropped lumps of clay and then smoothed them over.

There is loose rock called "scree" at the bottom of the Old Man of Coniston. When water freezes in the cracks in rock, it expands and breaks up the rock into smaller pieces.

Most of Britain's coal lies underground and has to be mined. You can usually tell a coal mine by the tower and wheel which work the lift.

This is Hay Tor on Dartmoor. It is made of granite which was pushed up, when it was molten, into the surrounding rocks. It gradually came to the surface as the top rocks wore away.

Prehistoric and Roman Britain

Prehistoric Britain

You can see many prehistoric remains in Britain. Prehistory is the story of man before written records began. It divides into three main periods: the Stone Age (3000 to 1900BC), the Bronze Age (1900 to 700BC) and the Iron Age (700BC to AD43).

Monolith (also called a Menhir). Single standing stone. Probably put up as religious monument.

Trilithon. Two upright stones supporting a third. Usually part of a stone circle.

Hill figures have been cut into chalk hillsides in some places. They may have been gods or emblems of tribes. Not all of them are prehistoric.

Hill fort. Hill fortified by ditches and earth banks. Built in the Iron Age, mainly in south of England. This is Maiden Castle in Dorset.

Stone circles. Prehistoric people built stone circles called "henges". They probably used them for measuring the movements of the sun and stars and for religious ceremonies.

Mounds and tombs

If you see a grassy mound like this one it may be a Stone Age tomb called a **long barrow.**

Inside long barrows are passages and chambers where people were buried.

Stone rings, like this, may have been entrances to burial mounds. They are quite rare.

Stonehenge

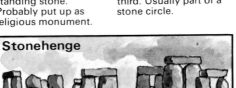

One of the most famous prehistoric monuments in Europe. Built over 4000 years ago on Salisbury Plain in Wiltshire. The largest stones reach about 7m above ground and 3m below.

Heelstone

Knob
Socket

On 21 June, the longest day, the sun rises over the heelstone and shines into the centre of the circle.

Where the trilithons have fallen down you can see the **knobs and sockets** which held them together.

A round grassy mound might be a Bronze Age tomb called a **round barrow.**

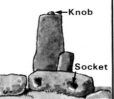
A barrow where the earth has worn away, leaving bare stones, is called a **dolmen.**

Silbury Hill in Wiltshire is a **man-made hill** built by prehistoric people. We do not know why they made it.

Tool marks. Simple stone hammers were used to shape the stones. You can still see the marks they made.

In the Orkney Islands there are the remains of a **Stone Age village** called Skara Brae.

You can see the remains of huts and courtyards at Chysauster, an **Iron Age village** in Cornwall.

Brochs. Tall, round towers built as fortresses in Iron Age. Found in Scotland.

Reconstructed farm

At Butser in Hampshire a research team has built an Iron Age settlement and is using Iron Age methods to farm the land.

Looking for flints

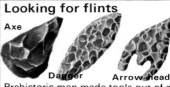
Axe
Dagger
Arrow-head

Prehistoric men made tools out of a hard stone called flint. Look for flint chips and tools if you are near prehistoric remains. They look like this.

Things to look for in museums

This page shows some things you might see in Prehistoric and Roman collections in museums. Many towns and archaeological sites have museums displaying objects found nearby.

Bronze Age clay beaker found in burial mound. These have patterns of lines scratched on them.

Iron Age helmet. Shields and swords from this period have also been found.

Roman glass is very delicate. Jugs like these were made by blowing hot glass into moulds.

Scenes from Roman life. This is a reconstruction of a mosaic craftsman's workshop.

Armour and
weapons of Roman soldiers. This model is at Grosvenor Museum, Chester.

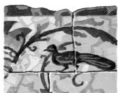
Roman wall painting. Specially good ones are on display at the St Albans Roman Museum.

Roman vase showing gladiators fighting. Many show scenes from Roman life.

Roman coins often have pictures of emperors' heads on them.

Sculpture and statues made by the people living in Roman Britain (left) were much rougher and less life-like than the ones brought from Rome (right).

How to find ancient sites

Tumulus (barrow)
Tumuli (several barrows)
Roman road
Earthworks
Ancient site

The above symbols and words are used on Ordnance Survey maps to mark the places where you can find Prehistoric and Roman remains.

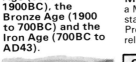
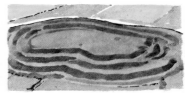

Roman Britain

The Romans first invaded Britain in AD43. By AD84 they had completed their conquest, although they never really controlled Scotland or the furthest parts of Wales. They ruled for about 350 years and you can still see the remains of many things that they built. This section shows you what to look out for. The map marks the main Roman towns, roads, villas and fortifications.

Villas

Roman villas were large country houses. There are several places in England where you can visit the remains of one. This is a model of the villa at Fishbourne as it probably looked in Roman times.

Mosaic. Pattern made of small pieces of coloured glass, stone or marble. Often used to decorate floors.

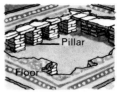

Hypocaust. Part of Roman central heating system. Space under floor heated by hot air from furnace.

Shrine. Many houses had underground shrines or temples where people prayed to their gods.

Towns

In a few places the remains of a Roman **forum** (market place) have been uncovered.

You can often spot a **Roman wall** by the line of red tiles running through it.

In some old towns you can see **Roman arches** and bits of their walls.

This is part of the **Roman Baths** at Bath in Avon, which were built above hot springs. They were rebuilt and used long after Roman times.

Look out for archaeologists at work excavating ancient sites. If they dig deep enough they sometimes find Roman remains.

Theatres

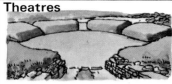

You can still see one or two Roman **amphitheatres** (circular arenas surrounded by seats), like this one at Caerleon in Wales. Here people watched shows, chariot races and gladiator fights. They also built semicircular **theatres**. The foundations of the theatre at St Albans are shown above.

Roads

Foundation Stones of Roman road. Roman cities were linked by long straight roads.

Very straight modern roads (not motorways) are often based on the foundations of **Roman roads.**

Milestones marked every Roman mile (1,000 paces) along the roads.

Hadrian's Wall

The Emperor Hadrian built a wall, 128km long, to protect Roman Britain against the warlike tribes who lived in Scotland. You can still see where the wall went.

There was a **milecastle** every 1½km along the wall, each defended by 50 soldiers.

There were 16 **forts** built at intervals along Hadrian's Wall and seven on the south side to give it extra strength. These are the reconstructed defences of the fort at Chesterholm.

Granary at Housesteads. Pillars raised the floor so that air could circulate and keep the corn dry.

Temple at Carrawburgh. Remains of temple where the Roman god Mithras was worshipped before the Romans became Christians.

Dover lighthouse

This is the only Roman lighthouse in Britain still standing. It was originally over 26½m high and fires were kept burning inside it all night. It is one of two which were built at Dover. The other one has now gone.

The Lunt Roman Fort

This is a reconstructed Roman fort near Coventry. Mock battles are staged here by a society called the Ermine Street Guard.

Saxon shore forts

Part of the shore fort at Richborough one of several built to defend the south and east coast against Saxon raiders.

Castles

There are hundreds of castles in Britain, varying from early motte and bailey types to huge palaces. This section is about older castles, most of which are in ruins.

If you are going to visit a lot of castles, it might be worth buying a season ticket. You can get these at many sites.

If you want to remember the castles you visit, it is a good idea to buy a guidebook at the entrance. If you take a notebook and pencil along with you, you can draw the things you see and make notes as you walk round (see opposite page for ideas). If you have a camera, take a few photographs too and afterwards you can put together a proper record of your visit.

Most English castles were built between 1050 and 1600, when kings and lords needed somewhere to defend their families against enemies. Many were altered and added to as designs changed.

Windsor Castle is one of the homes of the Queen and royal family and is the largest inhabited castle in Europe. It was founded by William the Conqueror, added to over the years and largely rebuilt in the 1820s. You can go inside the Chapel and State Apartments.

Things to spot at castles

Here are some things to try and spot if you visit a castle. Most of them are things that were useful for keeping out enemies, whose main weapons were bows and arrows, catapults, battering rams and siege towers.

Moat. Deep water-filled ditch surrounding a castle to deter enemies. Some have now been drained.

Drawbridge. Bridge for crossing moat that could be raised or lowered from inside the castle.

Portcullis. Strong wooden and iron grating for blocking gateway. Set in grooves so it can slide up and down.

Arrow slit. Hole in wall through which defenders could fire arrows without becoming targets for their attackers.

Gun-loop. After the invention of cannons, holes through which to fire them were often cut below arrow slits.

Murder holes. Holes in roof of a passage through which things could be dropped on to enemies below.

Machicolations. Holes in parapets or battlements through which stones and weapons were thrown.

Wall-walks between towers gave soldiers a good view of the countryside on all sides when they were on guard.

Spiral staircases, which wind around a central pillar inside towers, connect the separate storeys of a castle.

Fireplace. In ruined castles you often see fireplaces high up on the walls. This shows where floors used to be.

Beam holes. Sometimes in ruined castles you can see the holes where the beams that held up the ceilings fitted.

Early castles were built on a mound called a **motte** with a courtyard called a **bailey** at the bottom.

Most early stone castles had a **square keep** (main building) like this one at Rochester Castle.

Round keeps, like this, were built because they were easier to defend than square ones.

Later castles were strengthened by outer or curtain walls. These are called **concentric castles**. Edward I built eight of them in Wales.

Henry VIII built a chain of **rose-shaped castles** along the coast to protect England from invasion. This is Deal Castle.

Most castles were built of stone but in the last years of castle building a few **brick castles** were built.

In the 1800s it was fashionable to build houses that looked like castles. These are called **Gothic castles**.

Many **Scottish castles** are really fortified houses with the main living rooms on the upper floors.

Sham castles, like Mow Cop castle in Cheshire were built to provide romantic views rather than to be lived in.

Jousting

At some castles, in the summer, people dress up as knights and have mock battles. To find out where jousts are being held, contact the British Jousting Centre, Tapeley Park, Instow, Devon.

Armour and weapons

Look out for these on display at castles.

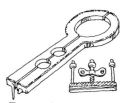

Suit of armour

Cannon

Crossbow

Here are some examples of siege weapons that were used to attack castles.

The **battering ram** – a tree trunk with an iron cap on one end – was swung on ropes against doors or walls.

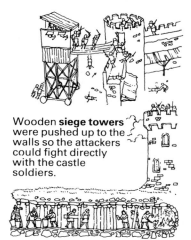

Wooden **siege towers** were pushed up to the walls so the attackers could fight directly with the castle soldiers.

Dungeons

THOMAS

In some castles you can visit the **dungeons**. They are usually underground and very dark and damp.

Torture instruments, like these thumb screws and iron collar, were used to punish prisoners.

Sometimes you can see the **names and dates** of prisoners scratched on the walls of dungeons.

The **mangonel** was a catapult used to throw stones and other heavy missiles.

Attackers often dug **tunnels** under the foundations of a tower. When the props of the tunnel were set alight, the tunnel collapsed and brought the tower down with it.

Visiting a castle

History. Find out who built the castle and when. Who is the owner today? Have any famous people been associated with it? There may be an effigy of the owner in the local church or a portrait in the local museum. Finally, try to find out why the castle fell into disuse.

Site. Look at the castle's position. Is it built on a hill, in an old town, by a river, on the coast, in open country? The site will give you a clue as to why the castle was built in the first place and what it was defending.

Defence. Walk round the castle and see how good the defences were. Is there a moat? Could the stream feeding it be easily diverted? Is there any high ground nearby from which a stone-throwing machine could pound the walls?

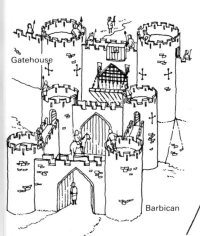

Gatehouse

Barbican

Entrance. What is the gatehouse like? Is there a barbican? A drawbridge? A portcullis? If not, are there any clues to tell you they were once there? Are there grooves in the gateway that held a portcullis, or machinery for a drawbridge?

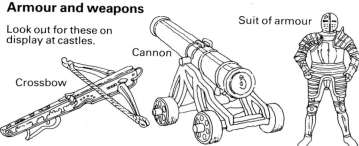

Framlingham Castle, Suffolk.

HISTORY – Begun in 1100. Improved over the centuries by the Howard family, dukes of Norfolk, who were given the castle in 1397. There are tombs of the dukes in the local church. Mary Tudor was living here when she was proclaimed queen. In 1636 the castle was given to Pembroke College, Cambridge, and most internal buildings were pulled down.

SITE – On a large mound. Built to protect the surrounding countryside.

DEFENCE – Dry ditch and outer moat, originally fed by the River Ore.

Tomb of Howard family

ENTRANCE – Large gatehouse. Original drawbridge over dry ditch now gone.

CURTAIN WALL – High curtain wall with 13 towers, mostly square. Spiral stairs. Many fireplaces and latrines. Good field of fire from wall-walk.

INTERNAL BUILDINGS – No keep. The only building left inside is a poor house, built about 1730, on the site of the great hall.

CHANGES – Tudor brick chimneys added in reign of Henry VII.

WEAPONS – No weapons on show, but tombs in church show Howards in armour.

Brick chimneys

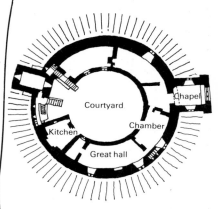

Curtain wall. Walk round the wall and see how good a field of fire there is on to the surrounding countryside. How easy is it to get to the wall-walks from the curtain wall? How many wall towers are there? Are any of them named? Are they square or round? Do they have spiral stairs? Do the rooms in them have fireplaces?

Courtyard

Chapel

Kitchen

Chamber

Great hall

Plan of a keep

Internal buildings. Is there a keep? What shape is it? Look at a plan if you can. How many rooms were there? Did it have a hall, chapel or kitchen? Look up: can you tell how many floors there were by beam holes, fireplaces or windows?

Changes. Look for any later changes to the castle. Have the buildings been heightened? Have any comforts been added, like brick chimneys? Have windows replaced arrow slits?

Weapons. Note down any weapons that are on display. In the local church there may be a brass of a knight in armour you can rub (see page 17).

15

Churches

Looking round churches can be fun if you have things to look out for. On the next pages, you will find some clues to the age of a church, a selection of things to spot in them and some information about different types of churches. Before you go into a church to look round it, make sure there is not a service in progress. There are usually several services on Sundays.

Cathedrals

A **cathedral** is a large church which contains the throne of a bishop or archbishop. There are 56 in Britain, many of which are famous for their architecture.

The **West Front** is often elaborately decorated with stone carvings.

The clergymen who run the cathedral have meetings in the **chapter house**.

See if you can find the **bishop's throne** or *cathedra* (Greek word for seat).

Cathedrals that were once monastery churches have **cloisters**. These are covered arcades round a square where the monks could walk and meditate.

Some churches were once part of a monastery or convent and the old name of abbey is still used for a few, like Bath Abbey. Others are now called cathedrals.

Ruined abbeys

There are many ruined abbeys (once monasteries and convents) in Britain. Most of them were destroyed by Henry VIII between 1536 and 1540, when he broke away from the Catholic Church.

If you visit a **ruined abbey,** see if you can find the part where the monks slept (the dormitory) and where they ate (the refectory). There is usually a plan of how it used to look on a notice board or in a guide book.

Churches

There are over 19,000 parish churches in Britain. In many towns and villages, the church is the oldest building. For centuries, it was the centre of the community and so it can tell you a lot about local history.

Look out for yew trees in the churchyard. They may be even older than the church. Also look for a weathervane on the steeple. The most common is a cock, the symbol of St Peter.

Chapels

Large churches often have several chapels in them. The **lady chapel** is usually behind the main altar.

Chantry chapels, often with railings round them, were paid for by people who wanted prayers said for them.

Regimental chapels are for the special use of an army regiment. They usually have the regiment's flag in them.

Sometimes chapels were built in remote areas because the main church was too far away. These are called **chapels of ease**.

Some independent religious groups, like the Methodists, call their places of worship **chapels**.

Organs

Organs have been used in churches for hundreds of years, but for a long time only important churches had them. Until the middle of the last century smaller churches used a band of musicians playing recorders, fiddles and cellos.

The organ is usually in a loft or gallery. Look for the long pipes. Each one plays a different note when air is let in.

The organist has keyboards and a panel of stops to work with his hands, and pedals for his feet.

Clues to the age of a church

You can tell from the style in which a church is built roughly how old it is, although some churches have been restored and added to in a mixture of styles. Here are the names of the main styles used in the Middle Ages, when most British churches were built.

Norman	1066-1189
Early English ⎫	1189-1307
Decorated ⎬ Gothic	1307-1327
Perpendicular ⎭	1327-1509

To date a church, try matching its doors, windows and overall shape to the pictures below. You will also see Gothic features in Victorian churches (1837-1901). These are often built of brick, so they are fairly easy to spot.

Doors

Round arch — **Norman**
Pointed arch — **Early English**
Arch less sharply pointed — **Decorated**
Square frame above arch — **Perpendicular**

Towers and spires

Low, square tower — **Norman**
Tall spire — **Early English**
Sharply pointed spire — **Decorated**
Tall, square tower — **Perpendicular**

Windows

Round arch — **Norman**
Pointed arch — **Early English**
Elaborate stone patterns — **Decorated**
Delicate stone patterns — **Perpendicular**

Things to Spot in Churches

Gargoyle. Stone spout to keep water from gutter clear of wall. Usually carved in the shape of an ugly head.

Flying buttresses. Arches on the outside of a building which act as props to hold the walls in place.

Sanctuary door knocker. In the Middle Ages, anyone who touched it could claim sanctuary and be safe from arrest.

Crypt. Underground room beneath most cathedrals and large churches. People were sometimes buried here.

Eagle lectern. Wood or brass eagle with outstretched wings for holding an open Bible.

Carved font cover. Often so heavy it has to be lifted by chains (The font holds water for Christenings.)

Hammer-beam roof. Type of wooden roof that has no cross beams to support it. Often beautifully carved.

Fan vaulting. Stone roof with ribs branching out like the sticks of a fan.

Roof boss. Ornament placed where the ceiling ribs meet. Often carved and painted like this one.

Pulpit with sounding board to reflect the preacher's voice towards the congregation.

Pulpit with hour glass to tell preachers how long they have been talking for. Often, only the iron bracket is left.

Chained Bible. You can sometimes see Bibles that were chained for safe-keeping when books were very valuable.

Box pew. Pew with high wooden sides. You get in and out through a door.

Poppy-head bench-end. Decoration on the top of a bench-end. There are many different poppy-head designs.

Misericord. Hinged seat in choir stall for resting on during long services. The underside is often carved.

Tombs

If the figure on the tomb is a knight with **crossed legs** he was probably a crusader.

If the figure on a tomb rests his **feet on a lion** it means he died at war, if his feet **rest on a dog** he died at home.

The kneeling figures on this tomb are called **weepers.** They represent mourning members of the dead person's family.

Rose window. Round window usually filled with tracery (patterns made by thin strips of stone).

Squint. Opening in an inside wall which gives a view of the high altar, when it was hidden by a rood screen.

Rood screen. Carved wood or stone screen which separates the altar from the congregation.

Sometimes tombs of very holy people show a **skeleton beneath the main figure** to make people think about death.

From the 1540s onwards figures in casual attitudes became popular. A favourite position was **leaning on one elbow.**

Some early tombs have **niches for receiving pilgrims' offerings** cut into the sides.

Pictures in churches

In the days when most people could not read and write, painted, carved and glass pictures in churches helped people to learn Bible stories. You will often see **stained glass windows showing Bible scenes.** This one shows Adam and Eve with the serpent in the Garden of Eden.

In some churches, there are **pictures carved round the tops of pillars.** This one from Wells Cathedral shows a farmer hitting a fruit thief over the head.

Wallpaintings have survived in only a few churches. The Last Judgement, showing Jesus judging people's souls at the end of the world, is a common subject.

Church bells

Most churches have a set of bells hung in the tower. Each one plays a different note and bellringers ring them in changing sequences by pulling on long ropes. Look for the **bell ropes** tied up against the wall.

Brasses

You will often see brass plates, engraved with pictures of people, fixed to the walls and floors of churches. They were put up as memorials to dead people. You can take rubbings from them, but you must ask permission from the vicar first and usually pay a small fee. There are also several brass-rubbing centres where you can rub copies of brasses.

The pictures on **brasses** are usually of important people, like bishops, lords, ladies, knights and merchants. The oldest ones date from the 1200s.

To do a brass-rubbing you need paper, tape and heelball wax. First tape the paper down over the brass, then rub the wax over the paper until the complete image has appeared on the paper.

Roman numerals in dates

Dates on old buildings are often given in Roman numbers, like this: MDCCXLIII (1743). Here is how to work them out. I = 1, V = 5; X = 10, L = 50, C =100, D = 500, M = 1000. Where a number comes before a number larger than itself, subtract e.g. IV = 4 (5 — 1), IX = 9 (10 — 1). Otherwise add the numbers together e.g. VII = 7 (5 + 1 + 1).

Great Houses

England is famous for its great country houses. Some are still lived in by the descendants of the noble families who built them, others belong to organizations which keep them in good repair. Most are open to the public at certain times of the year. The houses on this page show how styles of architecture changed over the years. When you visit a great house, see if you can tell which style it belongs to.

Oxburgh Hall, Norfolk, is a fortified manor house built in the 1480s. Early manor houses often have a moat and strong gatehouse like this.

Blenheim Palace, Oxfordshire, (built 1705–1722) is in the Classical style, which was copied from Ancient Greece and Rome. This style has lots of columns.

Harewood House, Yorkshire (built 1759–1771) has a central building with "wings" attached at either end, like most large houses built in the Georgian period (1714–1830).

This is Longleat House in Wiltshire, one of the fine country houses built in the Elizabethan age (1558–1603). Many of these are built in the shape of an "E".

In the Jacobean period (1603–1625, when James I was king) brick was a popular building material. This is Hatfield House, Hertfordshire, which was built between 1607 and 1611.

The Royal Pavilion in Brighton is in a style of its own. The outside looks Indian, the inside Chinese. It was built for the Prince Regent, who later became George IV.

In Victorian times (1837–1901) many houses, like Knebworth House in Hertfordshire, were rebuilt in a style called Gothic, which was first used in the Middle Ages.

Things to spot in great houses

Minstrels' gallery. Balcony in Great Hall used by musicians who played at feasts.

Painted ceiling. These often illustrate myths or famous stories.

Secret door. Blends with wall so it is hidden when closed.

Family crests

Many families have their own coat-of-arms, something like this, which is passed down through the generations.

Metal stamps for making **wax seals** on documents often have the crest from the coat-of-arms on them.

Coats-of-arms are often used as decoration, specially over doorways and fireplaces.

Linenfold panelling. Design in wood pannelling which looks like draped cloth.

Fire screen. Used by ladies to shield their faces from the heat of the fire.

Silent companions. Painted wooden figures, usually by fires, said to keep ladies company.

Portraits

See if you can spot any family likenesses between the people in the paintings in the house. They are often ancestors of the family who owns the house.

Ghosts

If you visit an old house ask if it is supposed to be haunted. This is the ghost of Catherine Howard, the fifth wife of Henry VIII, who is said to haunt Hampton Court.

Four-poster bed. The curtains were drawn at night to give privacy and keep out draughts.

Basin and jug. Before houses had bathrooms, maids brought water for washing to the bedrooms.

Bellrope. When this was pulled a bell rang in the servants' part of the house.

Gardens

Knot Garden. Low box hedges divide the flower beds into elaborate patterns.

Topiary. Shrubs clipped into ornamental shapes, often of birds or animals.

Sundial. A shadow cast by the sun falls on a surface marked with hours and shows you the time.

Warming pan. These were filled with hot coals and used for warming and airing beds.

Spit for roasting meat over a fire. A boy turned the handle so meat cooked on all sides.

Mirror with candles. The light was reflected by the mirror and so made the room brighter.

Temple. At one time it was fashionable to build mock temples as garden ornaments.

Maze. Complicated network of paths with high hedges on either side. There is only one way to the centre and back again so it is easy to get lost in them.

Some country houses are still as they were built originally, others have been altered over the years. The furniture is often in different styles too. Here are a few clues to help you tell the age of the things you see.

Tudor and Jacobean houses 1480s–1625

The great hall was the showplace, used for entertaining important guests. The floor was made of wood, stone, or black and white marble squares. Look for wood panelling on the walls, or tapestries.

The long gallery ran the whole length of the house. Ladies walked here when it was too cold or wet to go out, and children were taught their lessons. Notice the wood panelling and the small-paned "mullioned" windows.

The Classical style 1625–1714

The Classical style was introduced into England by architects and designers like Inigo Jones. Arches over doorways (called "pediments") and columns were used to give an elegant, well-balanced look.

By this time there were many more rooms and they were smaller. One of the most important was the dining room. Thin wooden panels called wainscotting covered the walls, and the walls and doors matched perfectly. Ceilings were plastered or painted and floors carpeted.

The Georgian Age 1714–1830

Many large country houses were built in the Georgian Age, again in the grand Classical style. The main room was the great hall where guests were received.

Robert Adam was a famous architect who designed whole rooms to match, in soft, pastel colours. He often used the same patterns in his ceilings and carpets, and even in the furniture.

Trompe l'oeil

The main staircase was very grand and wide. Sometimes the paintings on the walls look so life-like you believe the people and objects in them are really there. This is called *trompe l'oeil* painting, which is French for "deceives the eye".

Many houses were built so you passed straight from one room into another, even from bedroom to bedroom. You can often look down the whole length of the house.

Houses were heated by coal, which burned in marble fireplaces. The mantlepieces were often decorated with Roman-style vases, which Josiah Wedgwood made popular.

It was in the 18th century that tea-drinking became a popular British habit. Elaborate tea tables, caddies and pots were designed and porcelain tea cups were used.

Furniture to look out for

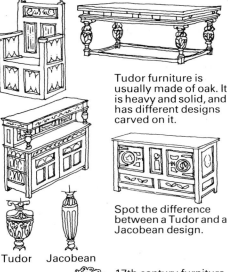

Tudor furniture is usually made of oak. It is heavy and solid, and has different designs carved on it.

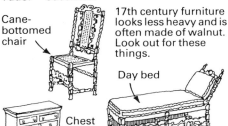

Spot the difference between a Tudor and a Jacobean design.

Tudor   Jacobean

17th century furniture looks less heavy and is often made of walnut. Look out for these things.

Cane-bottomed chair

Day bed

Chest of drawers

Gateleg table

In the 18th century mahogany was used as well as walnut, and lots of furniture was veneered. This means that a thin sheet of beautiful wood was glued on to furniture made of cheaper wood. Patterns were made by glueing veneers together.

Veneer

Veneered cabinet

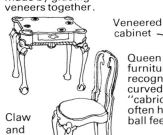

Claw and ball foot

Queen Anne style furniture is easy to recognize by the curved shape of its "cabriole" legs. These often have claw and ball feet.

There was also a fashion in the 18th century for Chinese-style furniture, called "chinoiserie". Sometimes people had whole rooms decorated in this exotic style.

Towards the end of the 18th century, pieces of furniture became smaller and more delicate, and legs straight and tapering.

Towns

Edinburgh, the capital city of Scotland, is built on hills and crags. This is Princes Street, the main shopping street.

York has many streets which were built in the Middle Ages and have changed little since then. This one is in the area called the "Shambles".

Bath. Famous for its hot springs since Roman times. Much of it, including the Royal Crescent (above), was built in the 1700s.

Stratford-upon-Avon. William Shakespeare was born here. This is the Royal Shakespeare Theatre where his plays are performed.

Chester also has buildings from the Middle Ages. The "Rows", shown above, are open passages along the first floor of the houses, with shops leading off them.

Warwick grew up around a castle. This 14th century building is Lord Leicester's Hospital, built for poor people to live in.

Oxford. Famous for its university. The round building is the Sheldonian Theatre, used for university ceremonies and concerts.

Cambridge. Also famous for its university. Here you can see people punting on the river Cam, in front of King's College.

Things to look for

Towns used to be surrounded by **city walls** for protection. In some old towns you can still see them.

City walls had **gateways** in them. These were the only way in and out of the town and were closed at night.

In the Middle Ages many town houses were built with **overhanging storeys.** This made the streets very dark.

Before tarmac and concrete, road surfaces were made of stones. Small irregular stones are called **cobbles.**

Gas lamps, made from ornate iron, were used to light the streets. Most have now been converted to electricity.

An **old-fashioned street name** often tells you what was sold in that street.

A **porte-cochère** (coach door) is an archway to the court-yard of an inn or house, wide enough for a coach and horses.

Old-fashioned shop signs showed symbols of the shopkeepers' trades. **Three gold balls** is the sign for a pawnbroker's shop.

Victorian pillar boxes have VR on them, which stands for *Victoria Regina* (Latin for queen). They are often six-sided.

Many town parks have a **bandstand,** where a band plays in summer. The fashion for these started in the early 1800s.

Local residents sometimes decorate their area with **wall-paintings,** on the sides of buildings.

Walls with stubs of iron on top once had railings. The iron was cut down and used to make weapons in World War II.

Things to spot on buildings

Mason's mark. When a stonemason worked on a building he often signed it with his mark and the date.

Link snuffer. Used to put out flaming torches, which were carried to light the way before there were street lamps.

Fire insurance sign. Showed which company had insured a building because each one had its own fire brigade.

Twisted chimney stack. Built in Tudor times (1485–1603). They are made of brick and are often patterned.

Blocked up windows. From 1695 to 1851 there was a tax on windows so people blocked them up to avoid paying it.

Wall anchors help to hold outside walls straight. They are attached to beams or rods inside the building.

Local museums

Objects, like these Saxon brooches, give clues about the people who lived in the area a long time ago.

Some museums have reconstructed life-like scenes from the past. At the Castle Museum in York, you can walk through 'Victorian' cobbled streets lit by gas lamps and go into old shops.

Tools and machinery, like this spinning jenny used for making cotton, tell you about working life in the past.

The houses of famous people are sometimes turned into museums. This is the room where Shakespeare was born.

Some museums produce leaflets which tell you where to go to spot historic things around town.

Different types of towns

When you go to a town, see if you can find out why it grew up in the first place, and when? Most towns started off as small villages centuries ago, but they usually developed where they did for a reason. Here are just a few examples of different types of towns with ideas of what to look for in them.

Norwich market square

Cathedral cities

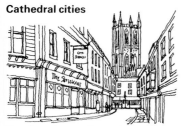
Butchery Lane, Canterbury

Any town with a cathedral is called a city. See if you can find out when the cathedral was built. Many medieval towns grew up round cathedrals and the oldest, most interesting streets to explore are the narrow, winding ones near the cathedral. Look for dates and inscriptions on the old buildings. Canterbury, Durham and Salisbury are examples of cathedral cities.

Market towns

Marlborough high street

Some towns had markets as early as the Middle Ages. Clues to look for are a very wide main street or a large square. Look out too for an old market hall or a market cross. See if you can find out what sort of market the town used to have originally and whether it is still held.

A market hall

Market crosses with shelves for displaying goods

Wool towns

Most of these are in the Cotswolds and Suffolk, which were important centres for the early wool trade. Wealthy wool merchants built many of the old buildings in towns like Chipping Campden and Lavenham, sometimes even the churches. See if you can find the merchants' tombs. Look out too for houses with lots of windows upstairs. These were to give weavers light to work by. You may also see inns called "The Fleece" or "The Woolpack".

Large windows
Lavenham

Sheep   Woolsack
Brass of a wool merchant

THE WOOLPACK INN 1455

County towns

These are where county councils have their headquarters. You can often tell a county town by its name. Leicester is the county town of Leicestershire and Ayr of Ayrshire. Take care, though, as this does not always work – Derbyshire's county town is not Derby, but Matlock.

Spas

Tunbridge Wells

Towns like Cheltenham Spa, Leamington Spa and Tunbridge Wells became fashionable because they had healing mineral waters. Look for elegant 18th century buildings, housing the baths and pump rooms, and see if you can spot "The Spa Hotel", "The Royal Pavilion" or "The Spring Gardens". There may still be somewhere in the town where you can taste the waters.

The Pittville Pump Room, Cheltenham

Industrial towns

In the 19th century, large industrial towns grew up around factories, mainly in the north of England, the Midlands, South Wales and Central Scotland.

Many of them have now been modernized, but you will still see smoke-blackened buildings, old mills with tall chimneys, and streets of small terraced houses. The finest building in an industrial town was often the town hall or the railway station.

Mill at Hebden Bridge

Outside toilets
Row of terraced houses

Manchester town hall

New towns

Modern new towns, like Milton Keynes, Runcorn and Livingston, were built to avoid overcrowding in other parts of Britain. They were carefully planned in advance with factories, offices, shops and schools. Look out for unusual buildings or sculptures.

The swimming pool at East Kilbride

Place names

Place names can tell you about a town's origins. The end or beginning of the name is usually the bit to look for. Here are some examples which go back to very early times.

Roman

-caster	}		
-cester	} fortified place	Lancaster	
-chester	}	Gloucester	
		Chichester	

Anglo-Saxon

-borough	}		
-burgh	} fortified place	Wellingborough	
-bury	}	Edinburgh	
		Shrewsbury	
-combe	valley	Ilfracombe	
-ham	small village	Chatham	
-ing	the clan of	Reading	
-ley	meadow	Chorley	
-stow(e)	meeting place, holy place	Felixstowe	
-ton	village	Kingston	

Scandinavian

-by	village	Derby	
-thorpe	small village	Scunthorpe	
-toft	farmstead	Lowestoft	

Scottish

Aber-	river-mouth	Aberdeen	
-an	small	Ardrossan	
Dun-	fort	Dundee	
Inver-	river-mouth	Inverurie	
Kil-	} church	Kilmarnock	
Kirk-	}	Kirkcudbright	
-ness	promontory	Inverness	

Welsh

Aber-	river-mouth	Aberystwyth	
Caer-	} fort	Caernarfon	
Car-	}	Cardiff	
Llan-	church	Llandudno	
Pont-	bridge	Pontypridd	

Irish

-agh	field	Armagh	
Bally-	path	Ballymena	
-derry	oak grove	Londonderry	
Don-		Donaghadee	
Down-	hill-fort	Downpatrick	
Dun-		Dungannon	

Longest place name in Britain: Llanfairpwllgwyngyllgogerychwyrndrobwllllantysiliogogogoch. This is a town in Wales, often abbreviated to Llanfair P.G.

Street names

Street names will give you lots of clues to a town's history. Here are a few of the obvious ones, but see if you can spot any that have more unusual meanings.

Baker Lane
Castle Hill
Wood Street
Oakdale Road
Victoria Crescent
Bishop's Avenue

MILL ROW

Population facts

Ten largest districts in Britain:

Greater London	6,794,400
Birmingham	992,800
Leeds	712,200
Glasgow	689,200
Sheffield	525,800
Bradford	468,800
Liverpool	462,900
Manchester	446,700
Edinburgh	434,500
Kirklees	375,500

Villages

Villages grew up in different places for different reasons. You can often tell from its shape why a particular village started where it did. Here are some examples. See if you can spot villages like these.

Some villages are grouped round a **village green,** which is common land belonging to the whole village. There is sometimes a duck pond in the middle. Finchingfield in Essex is a good example of this type of village.

Many villages are grouped **around a crossroads** because, in the old days, this was a good place to trade.

Villages on the coast are usually grouped **around a harbour or bay** instead of a green. This is Mevagissey, a fishing village on the coast of Cornwall.

Often a village lies in the **bend of a river.** Originally the river would have supplied water and been a good defence against raiders.

Some villages grew up **along a busy highway,** often a trade route. These are long and narrow. Broadway in Worcestershire is like this.

Sometimes villages grew up **around a castle or monastery.** At Dunster, in Somerset, the castle is at the top of the hill and the village is at the bottom.

In mountainous areas, like Wales, villages grew up **on the side of the valleys.** Many Welsh villages look like this.

Things to spot

Here are some things to look out for when you visit a village. Many villages grew up in the Middle Ages and some of the things you see will date from that time. Look out for dates on old buildings.

Manor House or Hall. Usually the largest house in the village. The lord of the manor used to live here.

Pub. Might be several hundred years old. Look out for a date on the sign or carved over the door.

Punishments in the Middle Ages

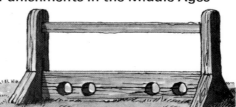

Stocks. People had to sit with their feet locked through the holes.

Whipping post. People were tied to this post and then whipped.

Old school building. Usually about 100 years old. Sometimes has separate entrances for boys and girls.

Almshouses. These were built by rich men as homes for old people. They are often long low buildings or rows of cottages, and have tall chimneys.

Ducking stool. Women who nagged were put on one of these and ducked in the pond.

Pillory. The lawbreaker stood on the platform and his head and hands went through the holes.

Lock-up. A small, solid building with no windows which was used as an overnight prison.

Other village things

The churchyard is often the oldest part of the village. Look at the names and dates on the tombstones. See which is the **earliest date** you can find. You might find several graves with the same family name on them.

A churchyard gate with a roof is called a **lych-gate.** "Lych" is the old English word for dead body.

Pound. Stray animals were caught and put in here. Their owners had to pay to get them back.

Dovecote. People used to eat doves (pigeons). They kept the birds in stone huts like this.

Tethering post. This was where people tied up their horses.

Crosses

Celtic cross. Often not cross-shaped, but has cross carved on. Very old. Put up by early Christians.

Market cross. Might be called a Butter Cross or Wool Cross, according to what was usually sold there.

War memorial. This is a reminder of people who died in war. See which war it commemorates.

Horse trough. Stone basin filled by rain for animals to drink from.

Pump. Water was often drawn up from underground by pump before villages had mains water supply.

Well. A bucket on a rope reaching down to the underground water. To raise it, you wind the handle.

Looking round a village

Little Bidlington in the Marsh is an imaginary village, but it shows you the sorts of things you might discover in a real one. Try finding out the answers to some of these questions next time you go to a country place.

1 Why did the village grow up in the first place? Its shape or position may be a clue. (See the top of the page opposite.)

2 How old is the village? Try looking for dates on the graves in the churchyard, on tombs inside the church and on buildings like the pub.

3 What are the buildings made of? Are most of them in the same material and is this local to the area? Notice the shape of the roofs. (See page 24.)

4 What kinds of buildings are there? Is there a manor house? An almshouse? A school? When was the church built and in what style? (See page 16.)

5 Are any names particularly common in the village? Again, look at gravestones, or signs over shops. Some families may have been there for generations.

6 If there is a pub, where did it get its name? If it is called "The Travellers' Rest", for instance, can you find out where the travellers were going?

7 Are there any particularly unusual things in the village with interesting stories attached to them? (See opposite page for some examples.)

8 What special traditions are there? Things like village fêtes and carnivals often stem from old customs and beliefs.

9 Did the villagers practise any special crafts in the past and have any been revived? Look out for a craft centre in places like an old mill or barn.

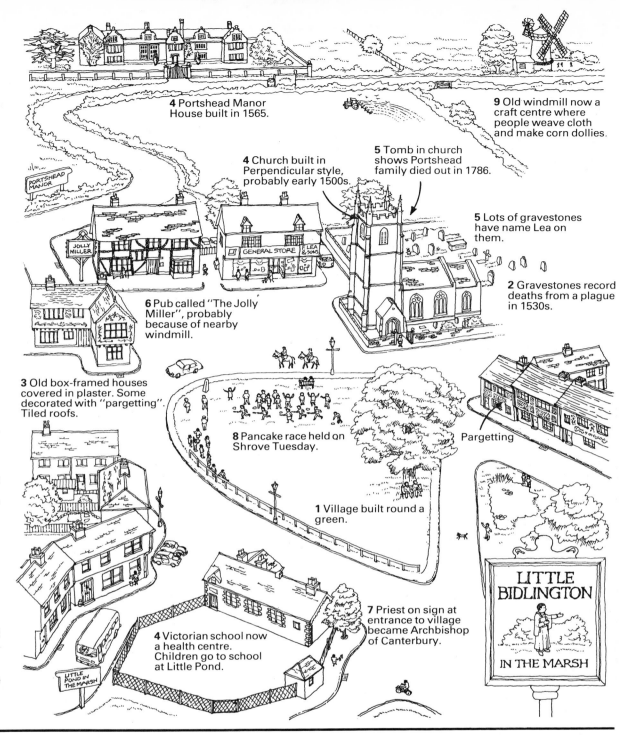

4 Portshead Manor House built in 1565.

9 Old windmill now a craft centre where people weave cloth and make corn dollies.

4 Church built in Perpendicular style, probably early 1500s.

5 Tomb in church shows Portshead family died out in 1786.

5 Lots of gravestones have name Lea on them.

2 Gravestones record deaths from a plague in 1530s.

6 Pub called "The Jolly Miller", probably because of nearby windmill.

3 Old box-framed houses covered in plaster. Some decorated with "pargetting". Tiled roofs.

8 Pancake race held on Shrove Tuesday.

Pargetting

1 Village built round a green.

4 Victorian school now a health centre. Children go to school at Little Pond.

7 Priest on sign at entrance to village became Archbishop of Canterbury.

LITTLE BIDLINGTON IN THE MARSH

Pub signs

As you travel about, it is fun to spot pub signs. There are thousands of different names for pubs, but here are some of the main types. When you spot a sign, see if you can tell which of these types it is.

A bush was the original trade sign for a drinking house. "The Grapes" and "The Chequers" are also early pub names.

Some pubs started as inns that provided food, drink and lodging for pilgrims, merchants and other travellers.

Sometimes pubs take their names from famous events. This one is called after Nelson's great victory at sea.

Some pubs are called after famous people. Dick Turpin was a well-known highwayman.

In country districts, you often see signs connected with farming or local trades and crafts.

Some pub names have a religious meaning. "The Star" gets its name from the Star of Bethlehem.

Many pubs used the name of the local lord and painted his coat-of-arms and family motto on the sign.

There are lots of pubs named in honour of the kings and queens of England.

You will probably see lots of pubs with the names of birds, animals and fishes.

Look out for pubs with names taken from a sport. These are not very common.

There are lots of pubs with joke signs. Here the "load of mischief" is the man's wife.

Houses and Country Buildings

Houses

Here are some old houses to spot. In the past, people usually built houses out of local materials and many areas developed their own particular style of building.

Rough stone walls and slate roof. You will see a lot of cottages like this in Scotland, Wales, Ireland and Cornwall.

Cob and thatch. Walls made of a mixture of clay, gravel and straw, called cob. Roof of straw or reeds.

Cruck-framed. Crucks are curved wooden beams which reach from the ground to the roof and support the house.

Box-framed. These houses are made of a wooden frame, painted black, which is filled in with plaster, usually painted white.

Limestone. This golden coloured stone is found mainly in the area called the Cotswolds. The stones are usually smooth and neat.

Flint. This is a very hard, steely grey stone, found in chalky areas. Flint houses often have brick frames round the doors and windows.

Tile-hung. Tiles are hung over wood and plaster houses to protect them from bad weather. You will see lots of these in Kent.

Weather-boarded. Wooden boards are fixed across the walls to protect them from the weather. You will sometimes see half-weather-boarded houses.

Roofs

Mansard roof. Roof with two slopes on each side, the lower one steeper than the upper.

Hipped roof. Roof with slopes on all sides.

Gabled roof. Roof which slopes on two opposite sides only.

"M"-shaped gable. Two gabled roofs side-by-side.

Crow-steps or corbie-steps. Step shapes at the end of gabled roof.

Dutch gable. Curly shape at the edge of a roof.

Thatch

You can see **thatched roofs** in most parts of Britain. They are usually made from straw, reeds or heather.

Look out for **bird and animal shapes** on the top of thatched buildings. They are often thatchers' trademarks.

Sometimes **church roofs** are thatched, though this is quite rare.

Notice board

Wall

Bus stop

Farm buildings

Here are some things to spot on farms. Some of them are old and quite rare.

Dutch barn. Open-sided barn used for storing hay and straw.

Old granary. Built on mushroom shaped "staddle" stones to keep out damp and rats.

Tithe barn. For storing grain paid to the church in taxes. A tithe was a tenth of each farmer's production.

Wattle and daub. Some old buildings were made by daubing clay or mud over a framework of twigs called wattles.

Silo. Airtight building in which green crops are pressed to make winter food for animals.

Oast house. Used for drying hops, which help to flavour beer. Many are now used as homes.

Cowshed or stable. The half-doors stop the animals getting out but let in fresh air.

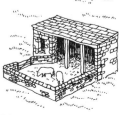

Pigsty. Place for keeping pigs. The shed has a small forecourt for feeding.

Henhouse. Sometimes on wheels so it can be moved around. The hens are shut in at night.

Beehive. Usually a white wooden box with compartments inside. The bees' entrance is just above the floor.

Windmills and water-mills

Windmills and water-mills have been used to grind corn for hundreds of years. People think windmills were introduced into Britain in the 12th century by the Crusaders, who saw them in the Holy Land.

Water-mills were built here even earlier, probably by the Romans. Both types of mill were in use until fairly recent times and you will see them in various parts of the country.

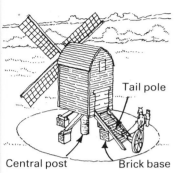

Central post — **Tail pole** — **Brick base**

The oldest sort of windmill is the **post-mill**, built around a huge wooden post, often a tree trunk. The whole mill revolved around the post so that the sails caught the wind. The miller had to turn the mill himself, or with the help of his horse, by pulling on a "tail pole".

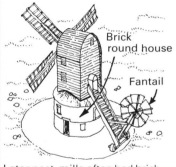

Brick round house — **Fantail**

Later post-mills often had brick round houses built round their bases for protection, and had "fantails" added. These are small wind vanes which pushed the mill round to the wind automatically.

Countryman's smock — **Fantail** — **Cap** — **Weatherboarding**

Smock mills got their name because they are shaped a bit like the smocks country people used to wear. They usually have eight sides and are made of wooden weatherboarding which is painted white or covered in black tar.

The sails were attached to the "cap" and only this part of the mill revolved. Sails were originally

covered in canvas and so the miller could still reach them to do repairs tall mills had a gallery round them.

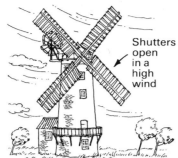

Shutters open in a high wind

Tower mills also have caps. They are usually bigger than post or smock mills, and are round and built in brick.

More modern sails had hinged shutters a bit like Venetian blinds. Old-fashioned sails sometimes used to get torn off in high winds, but now the shutters could be opened and the wind passed harmlessly through the holes.

Ogee — **Domed** — **Conical** — **Boat** — **Gabled**

How many different shaped caps can you spot?

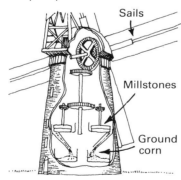

Sails — **Millstones** — **Ground corn**

If you go inside a mill, you may be able to see how it worked. The sails were attached to a series of wheels, and the movement of the sails made the wheels turn too. The corn was ground between two millstones.

First, the grain was hoisted up to the top floor, then it was fed slowly down through the millstones and into a bin back on the ground floor.

Windmills were also used to drain water from low-lying, marshy areas, and water-mills were used for many things besides grinding corn. They supplied the power for turning early textile and metal working machinery and were even used in making gunpowder and snuff.

Water-mills work in the same way as windmills, except that instead of the wind turning sails, flowing water turns a wheel.

Bridges

Clapper bridge. Very old type of bridge made of huge granite slabs resting on rock piles.

Hump-backed bridge. Steeply-arched stone bridge.

Bridge with "V"-shaped alcoves where people can stand to avoid traffic.

Iron bridge. The first ones were built in the early 1800s.

Suspension bridge. A roadway hung on huge cables from turrets at either end.

Cow bridge. Bridge for animals to cross, in places where a main road divides a farmer's land.

Viaduct. Arches which carry a road or railway line across a valley. This is Ribble Head Viaduct in Yorkshire.

Aqueduct. Man-made channel built to carry water. This is the Pont-Cysyllte Aqueduct in Wales. It is 305m long and has 19 arches.

Walls

Laid hedge. The young shoots in a hedge are woven round stakes to make it grow thick.

Dry stone wall. Has no cement between the stones. Needs great skill to build. Common in hilly areas.

Stiles. Steps over walls, fences or hedges. Here are four different kinds.

Crinkle crankle wall. Wiggles in and out. Found mainly in Suffolk, often round orchards.

Kissing gate. Old name for a gate swinging in a forked piece of fence. Animals cannot get through.

Cattle grid. Stops sheep and cows crossing but drivers do not have to open and close gates.

The **overshot mill** has water flowing along a channel above the wheel and falling on to its paddles or troughs.

Paddles

The wheel of an **undershot mill** is turned by the force of water hitting its paddles from underneath.

London 1

The capital city of Great Britain is London. It is one of the largest cities in the world. The oldest part, now the business and banking centre, is known simply as 'the City'. You can still see the remains of a wall the Romans built round it. London's famous shops, theatres and hotels stretch from the City to the West End. Here are some suggestions for things to do and see in London.

Buckingham Palace. The London home of the Queen. If the flag is flying on top it means she is at home. You can visit the Royal Mews where her horses and carriages are kept.

Trafalgar Square. Famous for its pigeons. On the column in the centre is a statue of Admiral Nelson, who defeated the French at the Battle of Trafalgar in 1805.

Piccadilly Circus is the meeting point of six main streets. In the middle is a famous statue of Eros (the Greek god of love) holding a bow and arrow.

The Houses of Parliament consist of the House of Commons and the House of Lords. Members meet here to discuss and pass laws. Big Ben is the bell inside the clock tower.

Westminster Abbey. Since 1066, all English kings and queens have been crowned here. You can see the tombs of most of them and of many other famous people buried here.

The Tower of London. Built as a fortress it later became a prison and place of execution. The Crown Jewels and a collection of arms and armour are now on show here.

St Paul's Cathedral was built to replace old St Paul's, which was burnt down in the Great Fire in 1666. If you go there, visit the Whispering Gallery.

A tour of Westminster Abbey

As you walk round the Abbey see if you can find the tombs and memorials of these people.

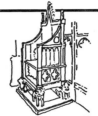

You will see the tomb of Mary Queen of Scots and other kings and queens in the Royal Chapels.

The Coronation Chair has been used at the crowning of English monarchs since 1300.

In the nave:
Robert Baden-Powell
Winston Churchill
David Livingstone
Charles Darwin.
In the north transept:
William Pitt
Robert Peel
William Gladstone.
In Poets' Corner:
Geoffrey Chaucer
Robert Browning
John Masefield
George Frederick Handel.

Mary Tudor is buried in the same tomb as her sister, Elizabeth I. See if you can find Mary's name on the tomb.

The Abbey Museum has wax effigies of famous people, which were carried at their funerals.

A tour of the Tower of London

Here are some things to look out for at the Tower.

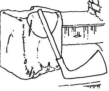

The Water Gate was known as Traitors' Gate, because prisoners were taken into the Tower there.

The axe and block, kept in the Bloody Tower, were used for beheading prisoners on the scaffold site on Tower Green.

The Crown Jewels belong to the state and are used by the royal family only on state occasions.

There are torture instruments in the Byward Tower. This cramp is called the Scavenger's Daughter.

The boy princes, Edward V and his brother, Richard, were probably murdered in the Bloody Tower.

Eight ravens are kept at the Tower. There is a legend that the Tower will fall if they leave, so their wings are clipped.

Ceremonies and uniforms

The Changing of the Guard at Buckingham Palace. The new guard, led by a band, arrives to take over from the old guard. The ceremony lasts half an hour.

The Changing of the Horse Guards at Horse Guards arch, Whitehall. This gateway is guarded because it was once an entrance to the grounds of the old palace of Whitehall.

Yeomen Warders (Beefeaters) guard the Tower of London. They sometimes wear blue uniforms.

Chelsea Pensioners— summer uniform. These old soldiers live in the Royal Hospital, Chelsea.

The King's Troop, Royal Horse Artillery. Can be seen firing salutes on state occasions in Hyde Park.

Getting around

This sign marks the entrance to the Underground (tube) stations. A quick and easy way to travel.

You can see more if you travel on the top deck of one of London's famous double-deckers.

If you want to take a tour, you can go in a special sightseeing bus with an open top.

A taxi is available for hire when its sign is lit up. Wave your arm to stop one.

Information services

Here are some telephone numbers you can ring for information about London.

071 730 3488	London Tourist Board
0839 123 400	What's On This Week
0839 123 424	Children's London
071 222 1234	London Transport Travel Enquiries
071 730 4812	Riverboat Information

London's history

1

The Romans founded *Londinium* in AD 43. The wall they built contained the town for 1,000 years. At the Museum of London you can see part of the wall with an explanation of how it was built.

2

In AD 61 Queen Boudicca led an unsuccessful revolt of native tribes against the Romans. You can see a statue of her on Westminster Bridge.

3

By the time of the Tudors, London had grown beyond the old Roman walls, to the west. Staple Inn, in Holborn, was built in 1586 and gives an idea of what London used to look like. Look out for other black and white timbered buildings. They are all in or near the City.

4

In 1666 the Great Fire of London started in a baker's shop in Pudding Lane and most of London burnt down. There is a reconstruction of the fire at the Museum of London. Afterwards, all buildings had to be built in brick or stone.

5

After the fire, Sir Christopher Wren was given the job of rebuilding St Paul's and the City churches. See how many different types of steeple you can spot. Today the churches are often used for concerts.

6

In the 18th century many houses were built in long terraces or around squares with a private garden in the middle. Originally these were the homes of dukes and earls, though some are now offices.

7

Many houses had wide doorways so that sedan chairs could be carried into the hall.

8

Today you will see many tall new buildings. The Barbican, in the City, was built on the site where the first bomb fell in World War II. It includes theatres, cinemas, a conservatory, flats and shops.

Famous houses

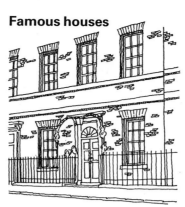

▲ **10 Downing Street** is where the Prime Minister lives. It is just off Whitehall.

▶ The Lord Mayor of London lives in the **Mansion House** during his one-year term of office. If you are in London on the second Saturday in November, you can watch the celebrations of the Lord Mayor's Show.

▲ **Lambeth Palace** has been the London home of the Archbishop of Canterbury for 750 years.

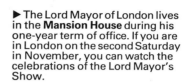

◀ **Kensington Palace** was the main private home of the monarch from 1689 to 1760, when Buckingham Palace was bought. Queen Victoria was born here and you can visit the state apartments.

London's horses

Wealthy people used to keep their horses in mews – stables at the back of grand houses. Many mews have been converted into houses.

London's police stations have stables for 200 horses. Police horses are named according to the year they join the force, e.g. all 1986 names begin with O.

In the Royal Mews you can see the Queen's horses and gold state coach used for coronations. It takes eight horses to pull it.

People ride for pleasure in Rotten Row in Hyde Park. The name comes from *Route du Roi* which is French for the King's Road.

Young and Co. is one of the breweries that still delivers beer by shire-horse and dray. The horses are black with white socks.

Troopers of the Household Cavalry exercise in Hyde Park every morning before riding to Whitehall for the Changing of the Horse Guards.

London 2

The River Thames

Hampton Court Westminster·Pier Greenwich
Kew Gardens
Charing Cross Pier
H.M.S. Belfast   St Katharine Docks
Tower Bridge

London grew up along the Thames and you can see some interesting places on its banks. This map marks the places mentioned below.

In the summer, you can take **boat tours** starting from Charing Cross or Westminster Piers.

The **Thames Barrier** is the world's largest movable flood barrier. It spans 520m across the river.

H.M.S. Belfast, one of the largest cruisers ever built for the Royal Navy, is now a naval museum.

The Cutty Sark, on show at Greenwich Pier, is an old "clipper" ship which used to carry tea and wool.

Tower Bridge first opened to let big ships through in 1894. Few come this far up the river now.

Ships used to unload at **St Katharine Docks**. It is now a yachting marina with a hotel, cafés and shops. There are lots of boats to see, including old Thames sailing barges and a lightship.

The Old Royal Observatory in Greenwich Park is where Greenwich Mean Time is measured from.

Kew Gardens have a vast collection of trees and plants. The glass palm house above, has exotic tropical plants.

Hampton Court Palace, built in 1514, is full of treasures and has lovely gardens, which include a maze.

Viewpoints

One way of seeing a city is to go to a high point from which there is a good view. Try to find some famous landmarks on the London skyline. Look out for St Paul's, Canary Wharf and Telecom Tower.

Primrose Hill. From here and from nearby Hampstead Heath, you can see right across south London.

Westminster Cathedral. Main Roman Catholic Church. Go to top of tower by lift for view of central London.

Parks

London is full of parks, gardens and green open spaces. Among them are ten big royal parks which were once the grounds of royal palaces. Many of them have boating ponds, lakes, playgrounds, statues and interesting birds and animals.

In **St James's** one of the royal parks, you can see pelicans and unusual ducks and geese which nest on an island in the lake.

This statue of Peter Pan stands near the Long Water in **Kensington Gardens** which join on to Hyde Park.

The Monument. Commemorates Fire of London in 1666. Climb up 311 steps inside the column for view of City.

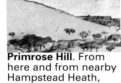

St Paul's Cathedral. You can walk round the outside of the dome, the top of which is 111m high.

Telecom Tower. Closed now to visitors, but you can easily see its unusual shape from most high points.

In **Richmond Park**, herds of fallow and red deer roam wild. If you are lucky you might also see a fox or weasel.

In the summer you can see performances of Shakespeare at the Open Air Theatre, **Regent's Park**.

In **Crystal Palace Park**, there are life-size models of dinosaurs on an island in the boating lake.

Interesting museums

There are so many museums in London that it would take ages to see them all. The British Museum and the Victoria and Albert (V&A) are two of the most famous. Here are some suggestions for other museums you might find interesting.

Museum of London. Illustrates the history of London. This is the Lord Mayor of London's state coach.

Imperial War Museum. Weapons, models, uniforms, photographs from all wars involving Britain, since 1914.

Natural History Museum. Dinosaur skeletons, fossils and stuffed animals, birds and reptiles.

Science Museum. Models and machines showing the history of science. Includes 'The Launch Pad' activities room.

Geological Museum. Gold, diamonds, precious stones, rocks and fossils and "Story of the Earth" exhibition.

Horniman Museum. Arts and crafts and natural history. These are from the musical instruments section.

Bethnal Green Museum. A museum of childhood showing old-fashioned toys, dolls and doll's houses.

Pollock's Toy Museum specialises in model theatres, dolls, teddy bears and other toys. It also has a shop.

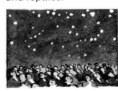

Planetarium. An audio-visual display of the night sky is projected onto a huge domed ceiling. Also a Space Trail.

Madame Tussauds. Life-size wax figures of famous people, including a Chamber of Horrors.

London Dungeon. Very gruesome displays showing gory scenes from British history.

Famous streets, shops and markets

Whitehall is where the main government offices are. The monument in the centre is called the Cenotaph.

Fleet Street is well known as the former home of the head offices of many newspapers.

Oxford Street has many big department stores and is probably the busiest shopping street in Europe.

Harrods is one of the most famous shops in the world. They claim they will get anything you want to buy.

Fortnum and Mason has an exotic food hall, selling food from all over the world. It has a special clock outside.

Hamleys in Regent Street is a famous toy shop which sells every kind of toy and game you can imagine.

Portobello Road Market. On Saturdays the road is full of stalls selling antiques and bric-a-brac.

Petticoat Lane Market is open only on Sunday mornings. It sells clothes and household goods.

Smithfield Market is the biggest meat market in the world. It is at its busiest in the very early morning.

Fun things to do in London

The Pirate Ships, 1 & 2 Tobacco Dock, E1. Tel: 071 702 9681 Two full-size replica ships tell the story of piracy and of the book 'Treasure Island'.

Rock Circus, London Pavilion, Piccadilly Circus, W1. Tel: 071 734 8025 Story of rock and pop music from the 1950s. Electronic moving, speaking, and singing models.

Guinness World of Records, The Trocadero, Coventry St, W1. Tel: 071 439 7331 Computers bring to life the Guinness Book of Records.

Cabaret Mechanical Theatre, 33/34 The Market, Covent Garden, WC2. Tel: 071 379 7961 Over 50 handmade workable gadgets.

Heathrow Airport - Terminal No. 2, Spectators Viewing Area, Hounslow, Middlesex. Tel: 081 745 5259 Views of main runway and Concorde in operation.

London Butterfly House, Syon House, Brentford, Middlesex. Tel: 081 560 7272 Free-flying butterflies in an exotic jungle setting. Insects include giant spiders.

Tower Hill Pageant, Tower Hill, EC3. Tel: 071 709 0081 'Time cars' take you back through the history of the City and its port. Display of archaeological finds.

Museum of the Moving Image, National Film Theatre, South Bank, SE1. Tel: 071 401 2636 Around 50 display areas with many workable devices. A cast of actors tell the story of cinema and television.

The Thames Barrier Visitors' Centre, Unity Way, Woolwich, SE18. Tel: 081 854 1373 Exhibition on the world's largest movable flood barrier.

City Farms include:

Kentish Town City Farm, 1 Cressfield Close, NW5. Tel: 071 482 2861 **Spitalfields Farm Assoc.**, Weaver St., E1. Tel: 071 247 8762 **Vauxhall City Farm**, Tyers St., SE11. Tel: 071 582 4204

Battersea Park Children's Zoo, Battersea Park, SW11. Tel: 081 871 7530 Open Easter - September.

Theatres include:

Little Angel Marionette Theatre, 14 Dagmar Passage, off Cross St, N1. Tel: 071 226 1787 Weekend puppet theatre with shows for 3-11 year olds. **Unicorn Theatre**, 6/7 Gt. Newport St, WC2. Tel: 071 836 3334 Plays for 4-12 year olds. Drama Clubs for 7-16 year olds and also Circus Club, with performances. **Riverside Studios**, Crisp Rd, Hammersmith, W6. Tel: 081 748 3354. Weekend children's theatre and cinema. Also theatre and circus workshops.

Street furniture

There are many odd objects in London's streets that are quite difficult to spot. Try looking for some of these.

Before free state schools, poor children went to **charity schools**. These had carvings of children on their buildings.

Blue plaques are put on houses to show where famous people lived. Charles Dickens lived at 48 Doughty Street.

Lions appear in many places in London. You can see sculptures of lions in Trafalgar Square and on Westminster Bridge, and lions' heads on the Embankment.

Shops with the **purveyors' sign** above the door supply goods to the royal family.

London has many **unusual clocks**. On Liberty's store, in Regent Street, St George chases the dragon on the stroke of every hour.

Many **bollards** are made from old ships' cannons. There is often a cannon ball on top.

You can see **animals on old iron lamp-posts** like these by the Thames.

Griffins mark the boundaries of the City of London.

In Piccadilly, near Hyde Park Corner, is the **porters' rest**: a shoulder-high wooden slab where porters could rest their load.

Metal plaques in the ground mark the route of the Queen's Silver Jubilee Walkway, made in 1977 to celebrate her 25-year reign.

The **Whittington Stone**, Highgate Hill, marks the spot where Dick Whittington heard Bow Bells call "Turn again, Whittington".

London Transport Museum

The transport museum, in Covent Garden, shows you the history of transport in London over the past 150 years.

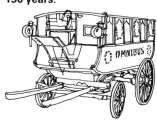

▲ You can see a replica of the first horse-drawn omnibus. Built by George Shillibeer, it made its first run in 1829.

▲ The first standard motor bus, the 'B' type, was introduced in 1910. Many were used overseas to carry troops in World War I.

◀ This Metropolitan Railway steam locomotive, built in 1866, was used on the Circle line of the Underground until the line was electrified in 1905.

Fun Things To Do

British Rail stopped using **steam trains** in 1968. But they have now become so popular that railway enthusiasts are allowed to run special excursions on main lines. There are also several private lines. This train is in Oakworth station on the private Keighley and Worth Valley line.

A **camera obscura** is a room used as a camera. Images from outside the room are reflected on to a table.

Cheddar, in Somerset is one of the places where you can see **caves** with stalagmites and stalagtites.

In **petrifying wells** objects are coated in stone by lime in the water. This one is at Mother Shipton's Cave, Knaresborough, (Yorks).

In Wales, there are several **small steam railways.** They run on narrow-gauge tracks and operate mainly in the summer.

There are several **miniature railways** in Britain, but the Romney, Hythe and Dymchurch line in Kent is the world's only mainline miniature railway.

The **Dr Who Exhibition** at Longleat has models and monsters used in the filming of the BBC television series.

At the **Dinosaur Museum**, Dorchester, you can see fossils, skeletons and life-size reconstructions of the dinosaurs' world.

Models of smugglers and an underground adventure with special effects can be found in **St. Clement's Caves**, Hastings.

There are several **old ships** you can go aboard. This is H.M.S. Victory, Nelson's flagship at the Battle of Trafalgar, at Portsmouth.

You can go for **boat trips** on most big lakes and rivers. Look out for the monster if you go on Loch Ness.

Watching people at work

Many factories and craft centres will let you come and watch people at work, but you often have to make a special appointment, well in advance. Local tourist boards can usually give you a list of such places. Here are some activities that you can usually go and watch without making arrangements in advance.

Several well-known **glass factories,** such as Dartington (Devon) and Caithness (Scotland), give tours which show you every stage in the process of making glass.

In **model villages**, everything is on a miniature scale, making you feel like a giant. At Bekonscot, in Buckinghamshire, the village includes a castle, a zoo and a railway.

At most **airports** there is a viewing platform from which you can watch aeroplanes taking off and landing.

You can often visit **potteries** and watch people making pots. Look out for signs as you travel around.

In villages, you can sometimes see **blacksmiths** at work, making horseshoes and iron objects.

Many **windmills** have recently been restored. Here at North Leverton in Nottinghamshire, the mill grinds corn.

Zoos and safari parks

There is a huge variety of bird and animal collections to be seen in zoos and safari parks throughout Britain. Here are a few suggestions for interesting places to visit and things to look out for.

At the West Midlands Safari Park you can see a wide variety of animals roaming free, including lions, tigers, elephants, baboons, zebra, camels and bison.

Most zoos have an aquarium, but one of the best is at Chester (the second largest zoo in the country), where you can see sea-horses.

Feeding times for the different animals are usually shown on notice boards. In Edinburgh, the penguins parade through the zoo before they are fed.

The Lions of Longleat is one of the few wildlife parks in the world to have white tigers.

Whipsnade Wild Animal Park has several rare species, including white rhinos.

Twycross zoo park has the best collection of apes and monkeys in Britain. These are rare proboscis monkeys.

Several zoos and safari parks now have dolphinaria where you can see dolphins performing tricks. They jump high out of the water and throw and catch balls.

Most zoos have a pets' corner or childrens zoo. These are special areas where you can get a closer look at the animals, and often you are allowed to stroke them.

Interesting museums

You may think that museums are boring, but there are lots of really exciting ones. Here are a few. Most of these specialize in a particular subject and in several you can touch the exhibits and even have rides on them.

The **National Railway Museum** in York has the largest collection of railway relics in Britain. Several engines are still in working order.

The **Museum of Costume** in Bath shows fashionable dress from the 18th century onwards.

Childhood Revisited, at Llandudno, has toys, over 1000 dolls, and a model railway.

The **Museum of Costume** in Bath shows fashionable dress from the 18th century onwards.

The **National Motor Museum** at Beaulieu tells the story of motoring from 1895 to modern times. Over 200 vehicles are on display.

There was once a famous ship-building yard at **Buckler's Hard**. Now its Maritime Museum displays models of the ships once built here.

The **Ironbridge Gorge Museum** is an open-air museum which covers the area around the world's first iron bridge. It tells you about industry in the past.

At the **Gladstone Pottery Museum** in Staffordshire, you can see demonstrations of traditional pottery making. The pots used to be fired in these "bottle ovens".

The **Boat Museum**, Ellesmere Port, has the world's largest collection of traditional canal boats. This unusual swan-shaped boat is also on display.

At the **Tramway Museum**, Crich, Derbyshire, you can see horse-drawn and steam trams and ride on electric trams. All of these were once used in big cities.

This old market hall is in the **Weald and Downland Open-Air Museum** in Sussex. The museum rescues and rebuilds historic buildings from south-east England.

At the **Beamish North of England Open-Air Museum** you can see cottages and farms as they were 100 years ago. There is also a steam train, an old station and a colliery.

The historic aeroplanes in the **Shuttleworth Collection**, near Biggleswade, are kept in working order.

The **Canal Museum** at Stoke Bruerne tells you about life on the canals. This is the inside of a narrow boat.

Old fire engines and equipment are on display at the **South Yorkshire Fire Service Museum**.

The **Musical Museum** at Brentford in Middlesex has a fascinating collection of automatic pianos, organs and music boxes. All of them are in working order.

The **American Museum** in Bath shows how people in America have lived over the past few hundred years. This is a full-size model of a native-American tepee.

Wildlife parks

The Norfolk Wildlife Park and Nature Centre has the largest collection of European animals, like this badger, in the world. It also has many rare breeds of pheasant.

In the Highland Wildlife Park you can see a wide selection of animals that either used to live in the area or, like this wild cat, still do but are not easy to see.

Farm parks

If you are interested in farms and farm animals, you might enjoy a visit to a farm park. At Easton Farm Park, Suffolk, you can watch the herd of cows being milked.

Many farm parks and farm museums show you old-fashioned methods of farming. Many things that used to be done by hand are now done by machine.

The Wildfowl & Wetlands Trust centre at Slimbridge has thousands of flamingoes, geese, swans and ducks. This is the brightly coloured mandarin duck.

Nature trails

Many parks and forests have nature trails which you can follow. Signs and leaflets tell you about the birds, animals and plants you might see.

Special collections

The Otter Trust in Suffolk protects and breeds otters, which are endangered animals.

You can see living butterflies and learn how to breed them at Worldwide Butterflies in Dorset.

The National Birds of Prey Centre in Newent, has regular flying displays.

Festivals, Shows and Sporting Events

Shows and festivals are often advertised on posters and in newspapers. Tourist offices and libraries can usually tell you about special events happening in their areas. For some of the big events it is best to buy tickets in advance.

The **Edinburgh Festival** is one of the biggest arts festivals in the world. It takes place every year in August and September. There are plays, films, concerts and exhibitions, and a military tattoo performed at the castle.

At the **Farnborough Air Show**, held every two years in September, you can see all kinds of aircraft. The Red Arrows give displays.

The **Royal Tournament** is a display of military skills, including competitions between groups of soldiers, held at Earls Court in London in July.

The Queen's official birthday is celebrated every year at the **Trooping of the Colour.** This is on the second Saturday in June at Horse Guards Parade, London.

The **Royal National Eisteddfod** of Wales is a festival of Welsh music and poetry. It is held in August and takes place in a different Welsh town each year.

Car manufacturers from all over the world show off their latest cars in October at the **International Motor Show** at the National Exhibition Centre, Birmingham.

County **agricultural shows** are held throughout Britain in the summer months. Farmers compete to win prizes for the best animals and crops.

Dancing round a maypole on 1 May is an ancient custom. Look out for it in country villages.

Morris dancers often appear at local festivals. They wear special costumes with bells on their legs.

Travelling **fairs** visit most towns during the year. Some places have a medieval fair in the summer.

Sheep dog trials test how good dogs are at rounding up sheep. National trials are held every summer.

Dogs of all kinds can be seen at **Cruft's International Dog Show,** held every January at the N.E.C. in Birmingham.

The **Chelsea Flower Show** is world famous. It is held in the gardens of Chelsea Royal Hospital in London every May.

Circuses began in Britain in the 1770s. There are now 23 circus groups which travel round the country giving shows.

On 5 November, people light **bonfires and fireworks** in memory Guy Fawkes' attempt to blow up the Houses of Parliament in 1605.

On Christmas Eve, **carol singers** traditionally go round and sing outside people's houses.

In Scotland, there are **Highland Gatherings** where you can see piping and dancing and athletic contests.

Rowing teams from all over the world compete in the famous **regatta** held on the Thames at Henley in July.

Veteran cars can be seen taking part in the R.A.C. London to Brighton Run in November.

Sports

The soccer (football) season lasts from August to April. The highlight of the season is the F.A. Cup Final held at Wembley Stadium in London in May.

Amateur, 15-a-side teams play Rugby Union and, in the north of England, professional 13-a-side teams play Rugby League. You can see both every winter Saturday.

Horse races are held all year round. The famous races are the Derby, first held in 1780, and now run every year in June, and the Grand National, which is run in April.

Britain's round of the world motor-racing drivers' championships is the John Player Grand Prix. It is usually held in July at either Brands Hatch or Silverstone motor racing tracks.

In the summer, county cricket teams play in various competitions, like the Benson and Hedges Cup and the Nat. West. Cup. There are also test matches against other countries.

The world's top tennis players come to Wimbledon every year for the Lawn Tennis Championships. They are held in the last week of June and the first week of July.

World championship motor cycle races are held at major race tracks. Speedway racing takes place most weeks. Check local papers for dates and places.

The main show-jumping events are the International Show-jumping Championships in December and the Royal International Horse Show in June.

The Seaside

1 Sea bathing was almost unheard of in Britain until the early 1700s. Then, doctors decided that going in the sea and even drinking sea water were good for the health and wealthy people started going to the coast. This picture shows Scarborough, one of the first seaside resorts, in the 1770s. The carts are bathing machines which were dragged out to sea by horses and used by people to bathe from.

2 In the early 1800s doctors discovered that sea air was healthy too. Elegant houses were built facing the sea and promenades were built along the sea front. Places like Brighton and Weymouth became fashionable when royalty went there. After the railways were built in the mid 1800s many resorts grew in popularity as more and more people were able to get to the coast.

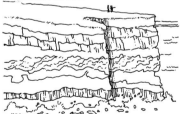

3 As early as 1800, people were amusing themselves on the beach by taking donkey rides, which were probably introduced by gypsies. Later, some beaches had carriages pulled by goats for children to ride in. Punch and Judy shows were also popular.

4 Piers were originally built as landing stages for boats, but they gradually became places where people went to enjoy themselves. Many were built in the 1880s and most had a pavilion on them with things like aquaria, flea circuses and souvenir shops inside.

5 There were penny slot-machines on piers from about 1900 onwards. A popular one was the electric-shock machine, which people thought cured various illnesses. **Remember When**, on Hastings Pier, is a slot-machine museum. You can borrow old pennies to work the machines.

Looking at rocks

The seaside is a particularly good place for looking at rocks. You can often see different patterns and colours in the cliffs and find fossils or unusual pebbles on the beach.

Fossils are the remains or forms of once-living plants and animals, preserved by minerals in rocks. Here are two fairly common kinds.

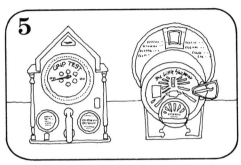

Ammonite

Belemnite

You can often see **layers** in the cliffs. These show they are sedimentary rocks, which were made under the sea.

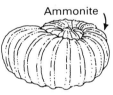

Look out for places where earth movements have made the rocks split and shift, causing a break or **fault** in the layers.

Movements inside the earth also make **folds** in the rocks. Upward folds are called anticlines and downward folds synclines.

In some places the sand is unusual colours. Alum Bay, on the Isle of Wight, has 12 **different coloured sands**.

Guarding the coast

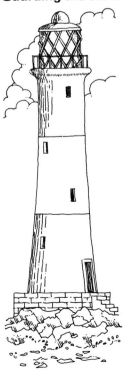

Britain has 209 **lifeboat stations**. You can go inside most of them and see the boat and other equipment, which are always kept ready for an emergency.

Look out for radio masts on **coastguard stations**. If a ship is in distress, it can send a signal to the coastguards and they will call out the lifeboat.

You can look round about a dozen of Britain's **lighthouses**. For a list write to: Information Officer, Trinity House, Tower Hill, London, EC3N 4DH.

Martello towers are round forts which were built along the south-east coast in the early 1800s, when people thought Napoleon might try to invade Britain.

You may see squat concrete buildings like this around the coast too. They are called **pill-boxes**, and were built as look-out posts during World War II.

In the Countryside

Although Britain has a large population for its size, there are still many unspoilt areas of countryside that you can explore.

Some of the best places to go are those which are looked after by organizations like the ones mentioned on this page. The addresses of the organizations are on page 79 and you can write to them for further information. National and regional tourist offices (addresses on page 79) will also give you details.

Remember, you always stand a much better chance of getting a quick reply to your letter if you enclose a large, stamped, self-addressed envelope.

National parks

There are ten national parks in England and Wales. They are all named on the maps in this book, and coloured in green. They are not like ordinary parks, but are large areas of open countryside, usually moorland, mountain, woodland or sea, but with whole towns and villages too.

Booklets describing the parks tell you about the interesting things to see and do, whether there are facilities for things like camping, pony trekking or fishing, and give you information on the parks' animal and plant life, geology and history.

For general information you can write to the Countryside Commission, or for details and booklets about a specific park write to the main information centre in that park.

You will see the symbols of the different parks on their boundaries, at information centres in the parks and on pamphlets.

Areas of outstanding natural beauty

In addition to the national parks, there are several smaller "areas of outstanding natural beauty" in England and Wales where industrial development is discouraged. These are marked in the same colour as the national parks on the maps in this book.

Forest parks

Scotland, England and Wales have fourteen forest parks. These are: Glenmore, Tummel, Queen Elizabeth, Argyll, Galloway, Border, Grizedale, Delamere, Dean, Thetford, New Forest, Snowdonia, North Riding and South-East Wales.

Their main purpose is to grow timber, but areas are open to the public for walking, camping, picnicking and often also for wayfaring, canoeing, birdwatching etc. There are signposted forest walks and nature trails. Details of these can be obtained from visitors' centres.

For details of forests all over Britain, write to the Forestry Commission, or, in Northern Ireland, to the Department of Agriculture (N. Ireland).

Country parks

These are areas of countryside usually near large towns. Some are small areas of wood or open parkland where you can walk or picnic, others have facilities for doing sports like sailing or riding and have museums or zoos.

For information on country parks write to the Countryside Commission in England and Wales, the Countryside Commission for Scotland in Scotland and the Department of the Environment in Northern Ireland.

The National Trust

Much of Britain's land is owned by the National Trust, National Trust for Scotland and the National Trust for Northern Ireland. The Trusts preserve places of natural beauty and interesting old houses and buildings.

There is a special membership scheme for people under 23, which gives you free entry to all the Trusts' properties.

Long distance paths

These paths have been planned so that people can walk through long stretches of countryside avoiding major towns and roads. Although it takes days, or even weeks, to walk some of them, it is often possible to go just a short way along them. All the paths are signposted with an acorn symbol. Write to the Countryside Commission for leaflets and guide books.

In Northern Ireland there is a 725km long footpath called the Ulster Way, which goes through all the six counties in the province. For information write to the Sports Council for Northern Ireland (address on page 37).

You can find out about organized walks and walking holidays on page 36.

Nature trails

A nature trail is a walk through an area with interesting wildlife or geology. You can often buy a descriptive leaflet, or there may be signboards to explain what you are passing.

Nature trails are marked on our maps with this paw mark symbol: 🐾 🐾 . For details of more trails you can write to the Forestry Commission, the Department of Agriculture (Northern Ireland), the Nature Conservancy Council (England), the Countryside Council (Wales), Scottish Natural Heritage, the National Trusts and tourist boards.

Here are some examples of the things you might see on a nature trail. These are taken from a trail in the Gosford Forest Park in Northern Ireland.

A "ha ha": a fence at the bottom of a ditch. It stops cattle from straying but does not spoil the view.

Small holes in the bark of sequoia trees, made by nesting tree creepers.

Moss growing on the north side of an oak tree, which is shaded from the sun.

Irish yews. The leaves and berries are very poisonous.

Poplars: matches and dart boards are often made from these trees.

Pond with different species of duck. This is a male mallard.

Traces of a volcanic rock called basalt, where the river has worn away the soil.

A badger sett. Look for tracks nearby and bedding piled at the entrance.

Sometimes kingfishers are seen on this section of the river.

A coast redwood. Coast redwoods are the tallest trees in the world.

A giant sequoia. Giant sequoias are the bulkiest trees in the world.

Many species of bird live among the trees. This is a long-eared owl.

Farm trails

These are rather like nature trails, but they take you around farmland so that you can see where the animals live and how the farm works. Farms you can visit are marked on our maps by this tractor symbol: 🚜 . Tourist boards and the Countryside Commissions can give you more information.

Nature reserves

Many areas have been established as national or local nature reserves. These are protected as they have rare or interesting wildlife or geology. Most of the reserves are open to the public, though there are strict rules about where you can walk so as not to disturb or endanger the wildlife.

For details of nature reserves write to the Department of Agriculture (Northern Ireland), the Nature Conservancy Council (England), the Countryside Council (Wales), and Scottish Natural Heritage.

Bird sanctuaries

These are nature reserves specially for birds. Rare species are helped to survive and all birds can nest and breed there. Some of the sanctuaries are marked on our maps with this bird symbol: 🐦

Many sanctuaries are round the coast or near reservoirs. Write to the Water-Space Amenity Commission for lists of reservoirs where you can watch birds in England and Wales.

The Wildfowl & Wetlands Trust runs refuges in England and Scotland for birds. You can watch swans, geese and ducks, some of them very rare, from specially constructed hides.

Pink-footed goose

Helping to conserve nature

If you want to learn more about nature and help preserve beautiful areas of the countryside or protect endangered species of animal or bird from extinction, you can write to one of the clubs and associations listed below. They are all different, but here are some examples of the type of things you can do by becoming a member.

Grey seals – an endangered species

You can go on field trips and expeditions to nature reserves and sanctuaries, learn about nature and conservation from newsletters and magazines, go on field study courses and holidays and, in some cases, help in a very practical way by doing jobs like clearing ponds, planting trees or making footpaths.

Watch Club
Wildlife Youth Service
British Naturalists' Association
National Trust
British Trust for Conservation
    Volunteers
Field Studies Council
Young Ornithologists' Club
British Trust for Ornithology

FOLLOW THE COUNTRY CODE

Guard against all risk of fire
Fasten all gates
Keep dogs under proper control
Keep to the paths across farmland
Avoid damaging fences, hedges and walls
Leave no litter
Safeguard water supplies
Protect wild life, wild plants and trees
Go carefully on country roads
Respect the life of the countryside

Outdoor Activities and Holidays

There are lots of sports and activities you can do outdoors in Britain, but it is often difficult to do them on your own. Here are the names and addresses of organizations you can write to for information. You will usually find it is best to join a club, where you can get training and sometimes go on courses and full-length holidays.

National and regional tourist boards (addresses on page 79) will also tell you which sports you can do in their areas and give details of special-interest and activity holidays.

Always remember to enclose a stamped, self-addressed envelope when you write off for information.

Walking

Many tourist boards produce good booklets describing walks in their areas, from easy, signposted trails to hill walks. You can get details of long distance paths in England and Wales from the Countryside Commission (address on page 79) and in Northern Ireland from the Sports Council (address on opposite page). For forest walks write to the Forestry Commission (page 79) or, in Northern Ireland, to the Department of Agriculture (Northern Ireland)(page 79).

The Ramblers' Association defends the right of the public to walk through the countryside and has several local groups. You can become a junior member.

The Youth Hostels Association provides cheap overnight accomodation in dormitories for people who are exploring out-of-the-way country areas. You have to be accompanied by an adult until you are 14.

Walking can be much more dangerous than it sounds, usually because of treacherous weather conditions. You should never set out alone. Remember to always tell someone where you are going and what time you expect to be back.

Addresses:

Ramblers' Association, 1/5 Wandsworth Road, London SW8 2XX
Youth Hostels Association (England and Wales), Trevelyan House, 8 St Stephen's Hill, St Albans, Herts. AL1 2DY
Scottish Youth Hostels Association, 7 Glebe Crescent, Stirling FK8 2JA
Youth Hostel Association of Northern Ireland, 56 Bradbury Place, Belfast BT7 1RU

Wayfaring and Orienteering

In wayfaring, instead of following a signposted path as on a nature trail, you use a map to find your own way round a specially laid out course, usually in a forest. Write to the Forestry Commission for details (address on page 79).

Orienteering is a more advanced form of wayfaring and you can compete against other people in trying to get round the course in the fastest possible time. Write to the British Orienteering Federation, Riversdale, Dale Rd North, Darley Dale, Matlock, Derbyshire DE4 2HX.

Camping

Camping gives you the freedom to explore out-of-the-way places and to follow your outdoor interests cheaply. The tourist boards can provide lists of campsites, but check before going to a site whether there is a minimum age for camping there without an adult.

The Camping & Caravanning Club, Greenfields House, Westwood Way, Coventry CV4 8JH, has a youth section for 12-17 year olds. Until you pass a camping proficiency test you can only camp on a limited number of sites under the guidance of a youth leader, but then you can use all the sites.

Special-interest holidays

There are special-interest holidays all over Britain, and the best places to get information from are the tourist boards. The British Tourist Authority, English Tourist Board and Scottish Tourist Board all produce guides to special-interest holidays which include subjects as different as mountaineering and landscape painting.

Holiday adventure centres

If you don't want to specialize in one activity, there are several holidays you can go on to try a number of different things. The guides to special-interest holidays published by the British Tourist Authority, English Tourist Board and Scottish Tourist Board include details of these multi-activity centres.

The Youth Hostels Association organizes adventure holidays covering a whole range of sports as well as walking. The minimum age for unaccompanied young people in England and Wales is 11, and 14 in Scotland.

If you want a real challenge, the Outward Bound Trust, Chestnut Field, Regent Place, Rugby, CV21 2PJ, runs adventure courses for young people aged 14 and over. Activities include canoeing, orienteering, climbing, caving, sailing and caving. The courses also involve survival expeditions in tough, outdoor conditions.

Pony trekking and riding

You can go pony trekking without having any riding experience. On a trek you go out in a group accompanied by a guide and an instructor, and the ponies go at walking pace.

At riding centres you get proper instruction in riding a horse (walking, trotting and cantering) and you can learn to jump and groom a horse. The following organizations have lists of riding and/or pony trekking centres:

British Horse Society, British Equestrian Centre, Stoneleigh, Kenilworth, Warwicks. CV8 2LR.
Ponies UK, Chesham House, Green End Rd, Sawtry, Huntingdon Cambs. PE17 5UY.
Association of British Riding Schools, Old Brewery Yard, Penzance, Cornwall, TR18 2SL.

Skiing

The place to snow-ski in Britain is Scotland. The season runs from December to May and there are five main centres. From west to east these are: Glencoe, Nevis Range, Cairngorm, Glenshee and The Lecht. Write to the Scottish Tourist Board for details (address on page 79).

There are also over 60 artificial ski-slopes in Britain, where you can learn to ski from about the age of 7. The centres are open all the year round. You can have lessons from qualified instructors and hire boots and skis. For a list of dry ski-slopes write to the British Ski Federation, 258 Main St, East Calder, West Lothian, EH53 0EE.

Archaeology

If you are interested in how people lived in the past, you might like to help explore ancient sites and record finds, before they are lost by being built over. The minimum age for helping on excavations is usually 16, though there are exceptions. The Council for British Archaeology, 112 Kennington Road, London SE11 6RE will put you in touch with your local society.

The Young Archaeologists' Club is an organization especially for 9-18 year olds. You can contact the club at Clifford Chambers, 4 Clifford St, York, YO1 1RD.

Climbing

Climbing is a difficult and often dangerous sport. It is unusual to take it up before you have had quite a lot of experience at hill walking or without joining a club. The governing body for the sport is the British Mountaineering Council, Crawford House, Precinct Centre, Booth Street East, Manchester, M13 9RZ.

Caving

This is another exciting sport that it is impossible to do safely without joining a club. The main caving areas in Britain are Derbyshire, the Northern Pennines, South Wales and the Mendip Hills. For information, write to the National Caving Association, Monomark House, 27 Old Gloucester St, London, WC1N 3XX.

Fishing

You can fish anywhere off the coast of Britain, providing it is safe. Sometimes you can go out on fishing trips with local fishermen. However, there are very complicated rules and regulations about fishing on inland waters and for this it is best to join a club which has its own stretch of water. Fishing-tackle shops are often the best places to go to for preliminary advice, and the Scottish, Welsh and Northern Ireland Tourist Boards all produce good fishing guides.

Other useful addresses:

The National Federation of Anglers, Halliday House, 2 Wilson St, Derbyshire, DE1 1PG
Salmon and Trout Association, Fishmonger's Hall, London Bridge, London EC4R 9EL

Golf

Many golf clubs have junior members or accept visiting players, but if you are a beginner you might prefer to play on a public course. There are about 200 public courses in England and Wales where you can play if you are 8 or over. Write to the National Association of Public Golf Courses, 35 Sinclair Grove, London, NW11 9JH.

The Scottish Tourist Board produces a booklet with details of about 400 courses and clubs which welcome visitors and the Northern Ireland Tourist Board will also advise you on playing golf in Ulster (addresses on page 79).

Cycling

There are two main sorts of cycling - touring and racing. If you are interested in going touring, write to the Cyclists' Touring Club, Cotterell House, 69 Meadrow, Godalming, Surrey GU7 3HS. To get involved in racing write to the British Cycling Federation, 36 Rokingham Rd, Kettering, Northants NN16 8HG.

Air-sports

There is a minimum age for doing most air-sports. You have to be 17 to fly an aeroplane solo, and 16 for gliding, parachuting or hang gliding. Parascending is an exception and you can usually start this at about 14.

In parascending you are towed along by a landrover, or a boat, wearing an open parachute which lifts you into the air. You then let go of the tow line and come back down to the ground as though you were parachuting.

British Gliding Association, Kimberley House, Vaughan Way, Leicester LE1 4SE
British Hang Gliding Association, Cranfield Airfield, Cranfield, Bedford MK43 0YR
British Association of Paragliding Clubs (including parascending), Old School Room, Loughborough Rd, Leicester LE4 5PJ
British Parachute Association, 5 Wharf Way, Glen Parva, Leicester LE2 9TF

Water Sports

Sailing

You don't have to own your own boat to learn to sail, or go on the open sea. There are sailing clubs all over Britain on lakes, reservoirs, and broad rivers, and most accept junior members. Write to the Royal Yachting Association, RYA House, Romsey Road, Eastleigh, Hants SO5 4YA.

Canoeing

Beginners canoe on streams or canals before trying fast-flowing rivers or the sea. Once you know how to canoe, you can enter competitions, for example, long-distance racing or rough-water obstacle-racing (canoe slalom). Write to the British Canoe Union, Adbolton Lane, West Bridgeford, Nottingham NG2 5AS. If you are an experienced canoeist interested in touring trips contact the Canoe Camping Club, 25 Waverly Rd, South Norwood, London SE25 4HT.

Surfing

Surfing is riding on an incoming wave either by lying or standing on a board. The best areas for the sport are the coasts of Cornwall and South Wales, though you can surf in other areas of Britain when sea conditions are right. You can hire boards at main surfing resorts. If you want more information, try writing to the British Surfing Association, Champions Yard, Penzance, Cornwall TR18 2SS.

Windsurfing

In windsurfing you use a special type of surfboard with a sail attached to it. This means you can use the wind as well as the water to move you along. You can windsurf both on inland waters and the sea. For more information write to the Windsurfing Department of the Royal Yachting Association at the address above.

Water-skiing

Water-skiing is similar to snow-skiing, except that you do it on water and are towed along by a boat. Unlike surfing, it can be done on inland waters. Most clubs have their own boats and provide equipment as well as instruction. Write to the British Water-Ski Federation, 390 City Road, London EC1V 2QA.

Sub-Aqua Diving

Swimming underwater is extremely strenuous. There are two main sorts of sub-aqua diving: snorkelling and "scuba" or aqualung. The snorkeller swims near the surface of the water, breathing in air through a tube, or dives as far down as he can holding his breath. The aqualung diver carries a supply of air in a bottle on his back and so can dive deeper and stay underwater longer.

Training in both sports starts in a swimming pool, or at the most in a very sheltered outdoor pool or cove. You first have to pass a test in basic swimming and get a medical certificate to show you are fit.

The British Sub-Aqua Club is at Telford's Quay, Ellesmere Port, South Wirral L65 4FY. Anyone from 8 years old can join the snorkelling section. You must be 14 to become an aqua-lung member.

General addresses:

Sports Council, 70 Brompton Road, London SW3 1EX
Scottish Sports Council, 1 St Colme Street, Edinburgh EH3 6AA
Sports Council for Wales, Sophia Gardens, Cardiff CF1 9SW
Sports Council for Northern Ireland, House of Sport,
Upper Malone Road, Belfast BT9 5LA

Map of Britain

This is a simple map of Britain showing you a few main towns, airports, rivers and hills. The different colours indicate different types of land and important farm and industrial products are marked by symbols. The lines of latitude and longitude show you Britain's position on the globe.

Key to colours and symbols

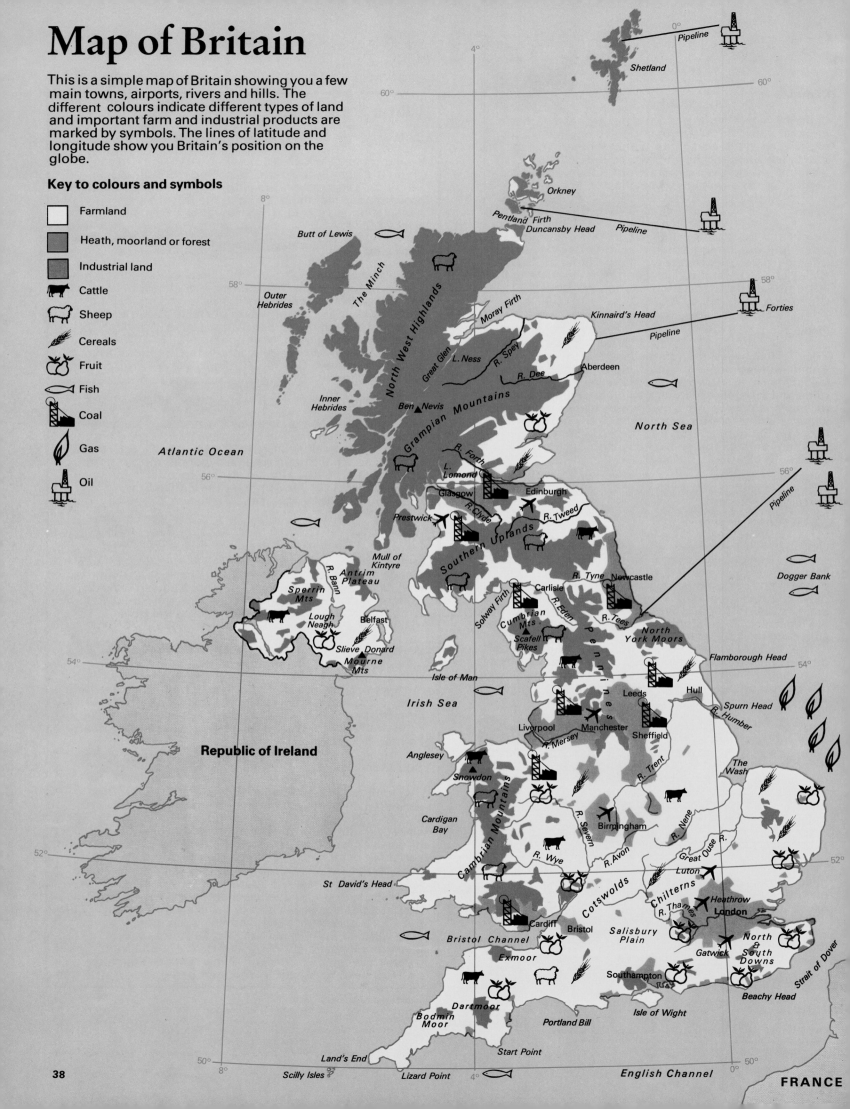

Farmland

Heath, moorland or forest

Industrial land

Cattle

Sheep

Cereals

Fruit

Fish

Coal

Gas

Oil

0°
Pipeline
Shetland
60°
60°
4°
Orkney
Pentland Firth
Duncansby Head
Pipeline
Butt of Lewis
8°
58°
The Minch
North West Highlands
Outer Hebrides
58°
Moray Firth
Kinnaird's Head
Pipeline
Forties
Great Glen
L. Ness
R. Spey
R. Dee
Aberdeen
Inner Hebrides
Ben Nevis
Grampian Mountains
North Sea
Atlantic Ocean
R. Forth
L. Lomond
56°
56°
Glasgow
Edinburgh
Prestwick
R. Clyde
R. Tweed
Pipeline
Mull of Kintyre
Southern Uprands
R. Tyne
Newcastle
Dogger Bank
Antrim Plateau
R. Bann
Sperrin Mts
Carlisle
Cumbrian Mts
R. Eden
R. Tees
North York Moors
Lough Neagh
Belfast
Solway Firth
Scafell Pikes
Pennines
54°
54°
Slieve Donard
Mourne Mts
Isle of Man
Flamborough Head
Leeds
Hull
Spurn Head
R. Humber
Irish Sea
Liverpool
Manchester
Sheffield
The Wash
Republic of Ireland
Anglesey
R. Mersey
Snowdon
R. Trent
Cambrian Mountains
Cardigan Bay
R. Severn
Birmingham
R. Nene
52°
St David's Head
R. Wye
R. Avon
Great Ouse R.
52°
Luton
Cotswolds
Chilterns
Heathrow
R. Thames
London
Cardiff
Bristol
Salisbury Plain
Gatwick
North & South Downs
Bristol Channel
Exmoor
Beachy Head
Southampton
Dartmoor
Isle of Wight
Strait of Dover
Bodmin Moor
Portland Bill
50°
Land's End
Start Point
50°
8°
Scilly Isles
Lizard Point
4°
English Channel
0°

FRANCE

Introduction to Regional Maps

The next 24 pages contain 12 regional maps. Each map shows one of the areas marked on this sketch map of Britain. All the maps are to the same scale and each one joins up or overlaps with the next. Notes round the edges of the maps tell you which page to turn to for the adjoining maps, so you can easily find your way from one to the other.

The maps show large towns and built-up areas, main roads, railways, rivers, farmland, woodland, national parks, and so on. The key to the colours used on the maps is at the foot of this page.

Interesting places to visit are also shown on the maps. They are marked with symbols and most of them are named. The symbols are explained in the key below. Note, though, that the maps are not detailed enough for you to be able to use them to get from one place to another. To find the exact position of the places mentioned you will need a good road atlas and sometimes an Ordnance Survey map too.

Many of the places to visit are also mentioned in the gazetteer on page 64, or are described elsewhere in this book. If you want to find out more information about them, the national and regional tourist boards can give you details. (See page 79 for a list of addresses.)

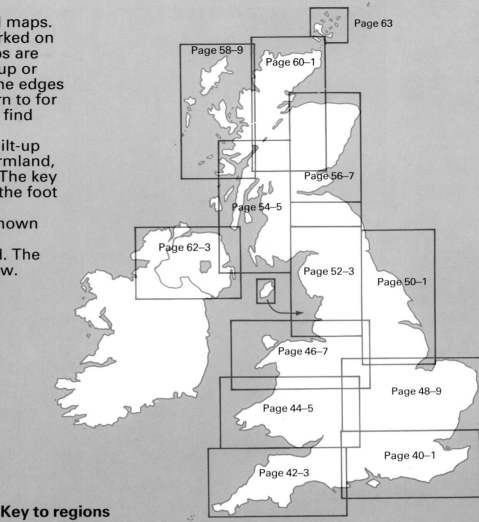

Page 63

Page 63

Page 58–9

Page 60–1

Page 56–7

Page 54–5

Page 62–3

Page 52–3

Page 50–1

Page 46–7

Page 48–9

Page 44–5

Page 40–1

Page 42–3

Key to regions

Key to map symbols

 Cathedral or abbey

 Castle

 Historic house

 Museum

 Roman site or remains

 Prehistoric site

 Safari park

 Zoo or wildlife park

 Bird collection or sanctuary

 Nature trail

 Farm park or farm trail

 Forest

 Fun thing (e.g. model village)

 Steam railway

 Old ship

 Airport

 Ferry

 Mountain top

Key to map colours

 Built-up area

 Farmland

 Woodland

 Moor or heathland

 National park or area of outstanding natural beauty

Water

Beach

County boundary

Railway

Motorway

Other road

Canal

River

South-East England

see page 48

You can look round the stables at the **Courage Shire Horse Centre** and see the blacksmith's shop.

Mapledurham is an Elizabethan mansion by the Thames. There is a watermill nearby, where corn is ground.

The Iron Age Celts may have cut this **White Horse** into the chalk hillside of the Berkshire Downs.

At **Marwell Zoo Park** there are open areas where you can watch lions, tigers, rhinos and giraffes.

see page 45

see page 43

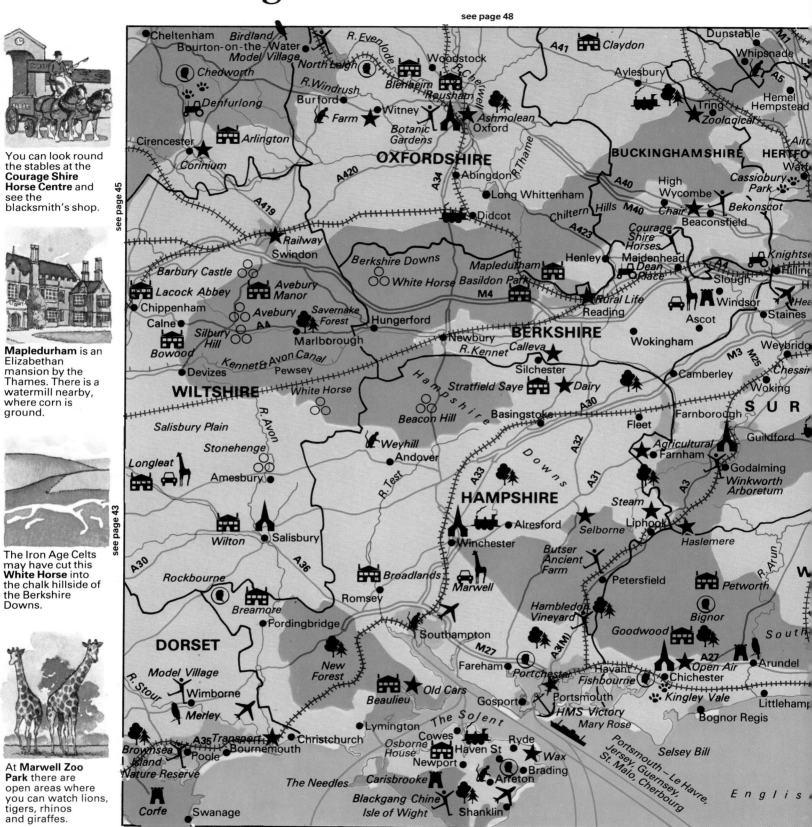

Cheltenham
Birdland
Bourton-on-the-Water
Model Village
North Leigh
Chedworth
Denfurlong
Burford
Witney
Farm
Blenheim
Woodstock
Rousham
Ashmolean
Oxford
Botanic Gardens
Cirencester
Arlington
Corinium
R. Evenlode
R. Windrush
R. Cherwell
Claydon
Aylesbury
Dunstable
Whipsnade
Tring Zoological
Hemel Hempstead
OXFORDSHIRE
BUCKINGHAMSHIRE
HERTFO
Abingdon
Long Whittenham
Didcot
R. Thame
High Wycombe
Chiltern Hills
Chair
Beaconsfield
Knightsb
Cassiobury Park
Wat
Railway
Swindon
Berkshire Downs
White Horse
Basildon Park
Mapledurham
Henley
Courage Shire Horses
Maidenhead
Dean Place
Slough
Hilling
Barbury Castle
Lacock Abbey
Chippenham
Avebury Manor
Avebury
Savernake Forest
Hungerford
Newbury
Calleva
Reading
Rural Life
Ascot
Windsor
Staines
Hea
Calne
Bowood
Silbury Hill
Marlborough
BERKSHIRE
R. Kennet
Silchester
Wokingham
Weybrid
Devizes
Pewsey
Kennet & Avon Canal
WILTSHIRE
White Horse
Stratfield Saye
Dairy
Camberley
Woking
SUR
Salisbury Plain
R. Avon
Beacon Hill
Basingstoke
Fleet
Farnborough
Chessi
Stonehenge
Weyhill
Andover
R. Test
Agricultural Farnham
Guildford
Longleat
Amesbury
HAMPSHIRE
Steam
Liphook
Godalming
Winkworth Arboretum
Wilton
Salisbury
Alresford
Selborne
Haslemere
Winchester
Butser Ancient Farm
Petersfield
Rockbourne
Broadlands
Marwell
Hambledon Vineyard
Goodwood
Petworth
Bignor
DORSET
Breamore
Romsey
Southampton
Fareham
Portchester
Havant
Fishbourne
Chichester
Open Air
Arundel
Model Village
Wimborne
New Forest
Old Cars
Beaulieu
Gosport
Portsmouth
HMS Victory
Mary Rose
Kingley Vale
Bognor Regis
Littlehamp
Merley
Lymington
Cowes
Ryde
Wax
Selsey Bill
Christchurch
Osborne House
Haven St
Brading
Transport
Bournemouth
Newport
Arreton
Brownsea Island Nature Reserve
Poole
Carisbrooke
Blackgang Chine
Isle of Wight
Shanklin
Corfe
Swanage
The Needles
Isle of Wight
The Solent
Portsmouth – Le Havre, Jersey, Guernsey, St. Malo, Cherbourg
Englis

Salisbury Cathedral was built in the 1200s in the Early English style. It has the tallest spire in England.

Cowes is famous for sailing. An international festival is held every August and there is a national sailing centre there.

Portchester Castle was built by the Normans inside the walls of an old shore fort originally built by the Romans.

Fishbourne is the largest Roman villa so far discovered in Britain. This is part of the mosaic stone floor.

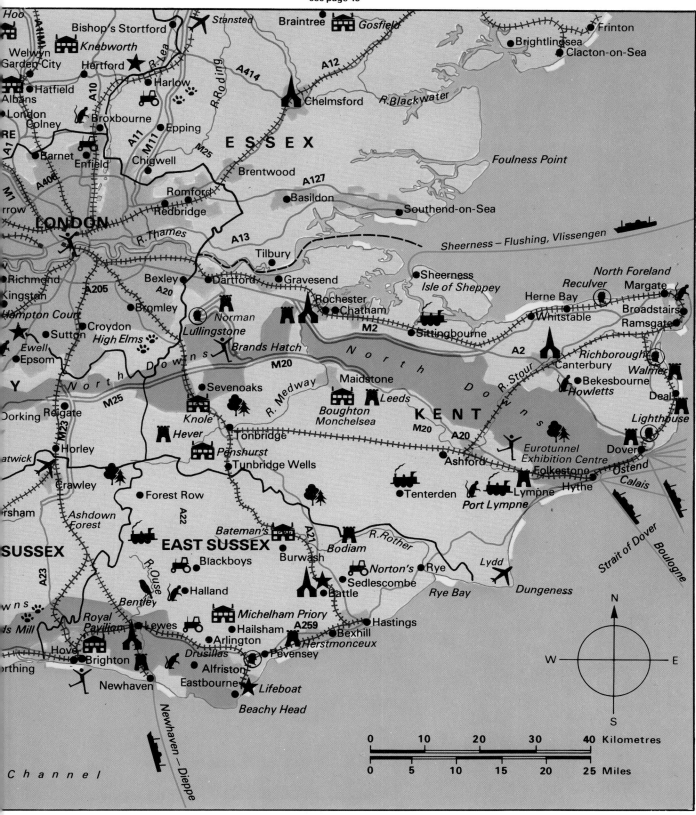

Map labels (clockwise/geographic):

Hoo, Bishop's Stortford, Knebworth, Stansted, Braintree, Gosfield, Frinton, Welwyn Garden City, Hertford, R.Lea, Brightlingsea, Clacton-on-Sea, Hatfield, Harlow, A414, A12, St Albans, A10, Broxbourne, Epping, A11, M11, R.Roding, Chelmsford, R.Blackwater, London Colney, Barnet, Enfield, Chigwell, M25, Brentwood, Foulness Point, A127, A7, Romford, Basildon, M1, A406, A13, Redbridge, Southend-on-Sea, ESSEX, LONDON, R.Thames, A13, Tilbury, Sheerness – Flushing, Vlissengen, Richmond, Bexley, Dartford, Gravesend, Sheerness, Isle of Sheppey, North Foreland, Reculver, Margate, Kingston, A205, A20, Rochester, Herne Bay, Broadstairs, Hampton Court, Bromley, Croydon, Norman, Chatham, M2, Sittingbourne, Whitstable, Ramsgate, High Elms, Lullingstone, Brands Hatch, North Downs, A2, Canterbury, Richborough, Walmer, Sutton, Ewell, Epsom, M20, Sevenoaks, R.Medway, Maidstone, Boughton Monchelsea, Leeds, KENT, R.Stour, Bekesbourne, Howletts, Deal, Dorking, Reigate, Knole, Hever, Tonbridge, M20, A20, Lighthouse, Horley, Penshurst, Tunbridge Wells, Ashford, Eurotunnel Exhibition Centre, Dover, Gatwick, Crawley, Forest Row, Ashdown Forest, A22, Folkestone, Lympne, Port Lympne, Hythe, Ostend, Calais, Strait of Dover, Boulogne, SUSSEX, A23, Bateman's, Bodiam, R.Rother, Tenterden, EAST SUSSEX, A21, Burwash, Norton's, Rye, Lydd, Blackboys, Sedlescombe, R.Ouse, Halland, Battle, Hastings, Rye Bay, Dungeness, Bentley, Royal Pavilion, Lewes, Michelham Priory, A259, Hailsham, Bexhill, Herstmonceux, Hove, Brighton, Drusillas, Arlington, Pevensey, Newhaven, Alfriston, Eastbourne, Lifeboat, Worthing, Beachy Head, Channel, Newhaven – Dieppe, Downs Mill

N E S W (compass)

Scale:
0 10 20 30 40 Kilometres
0 5 10 15 20 25 Miles

Look out for baboons in the monkey reserve at the **Windsor Safari Park**.

Southend-on-Sea is one of Britain's biggest seaside resorts. It has the longest pleasure pier in the world.

You can go on boat trips along **Regent's Canal** in London. Many go through Regent's Park to the zoo.

This is Queen Elizabeth I in the **National Portrait Gallery**, London, which runs special children's projects.

These chalk cliffs, near Eastbourne, are called the **Seven Sisters**. The dips on the top are ancient river valleys.

William the Conqueror built **Battle Abbey** to commemorate his victory over the English at the Battle of Hastings in 1066.

For several centuries the **Mermaid Inn**, at Rye, was a meeting place for notorious bands of smugglers.

The **Kent and East Sussex Railway** is an old steam railway. You can go for rides on it from Tenterden station.

South-West England

You can take a boat trip to **Lundy Island** from the mainland. 'Lund-ey' is the Norse name for puffin island.

Tintagel is said to be the birthplace of the legendary King Arthur. There is a ruined castle on the cliff top.

The clapper bridge at **Postbridge** was probably built in the Middle Ages for packhorses carrying tin from the mines.

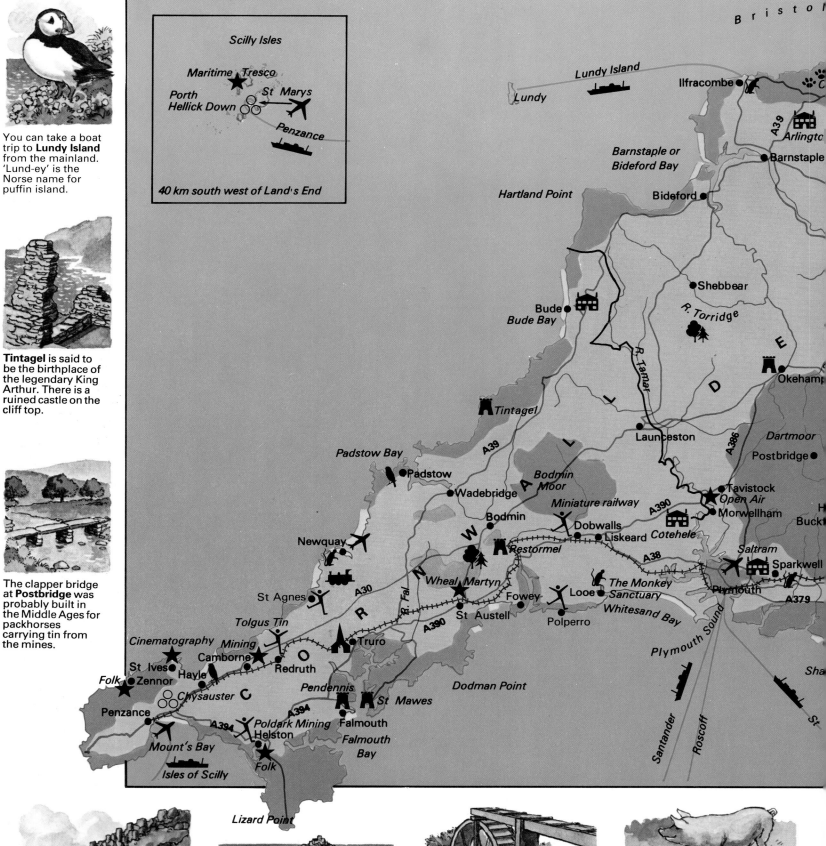

Scilly Isles

Maritime · Tresco
Porth · St Marys
Hellick Down
Penzance

40 km south west of Land's End

Bristol

Lundy Island

Lundy · Ilfracombe

Arlingto

Barnstaple or Bideford Bay · Barnstaple

Hartland Point · Bideford

Shebbear

Bude · R. Torridge
Bude Bay

D E

Okeham

Tintagel

Launceston · A386 · Dartmoor · Postbridge

Padstow Bay

Padstow

Wadebridge · Bodmin Moor

Bodmin · Miniature railway · Tavistock · Open Air · Morwellham · Buck

Newquay · Dobwalls · Liskeard · Cotehele

Restormel · A38 · Saltram · Sparkwell

Wheal Martyn · The Monkey Sanctuary · Plymouth · A379

St Agnes · A30 · Fowey · Looe

Tolgus Tin · St Austell · Polperro · Whitesand Bay

Cinematography · Mining · Truro · Dodman Point · Plymouth Sound

St Ives · Camborne · Redruth

Folk · Zennor · Hayle · Pendennis · Sha

Chysauster · St Mawes

Penzance · Poldark Mining · Falmouth
Helston · Falmouth Bay

Mount's Bay · A394

Folk · A394

Isles of Scilly

Lizard Point

Santander · Roscoff

These steep granite cliffs meet the Atlantic Ocean at **Land's End,** which is the most westerly point of mainland England.

There is a legend that **St Michael's Mount,** in Mount's Bay, is the tip of an ancient kingdom drowned by the sea.

Wheal Martyn Museum is an open-air museum showing the history of Cornwall's clay mining industry.

At the **Cricket St. Thomas Wildlife and Leisure Park** there is a children's farm with rare breeds.

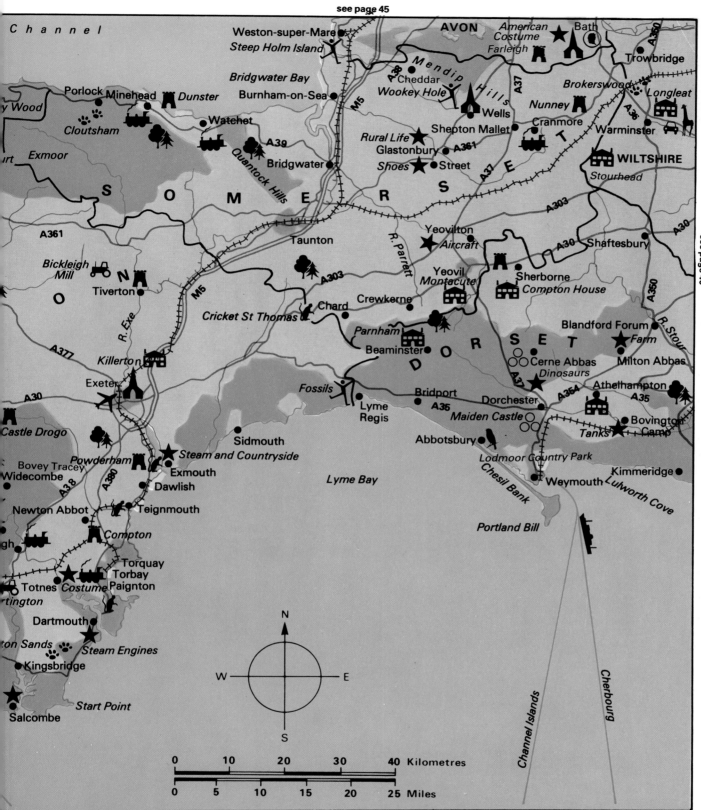
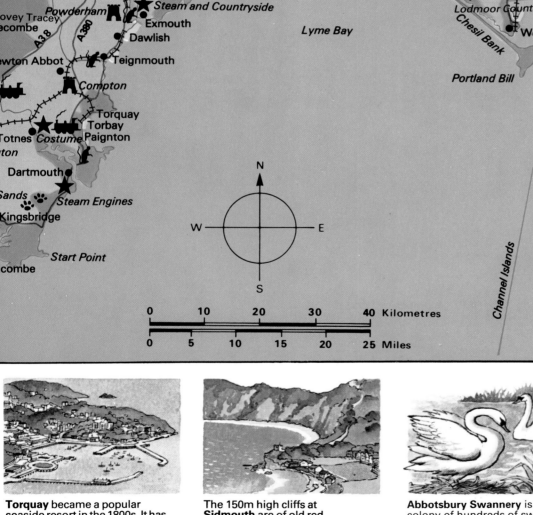

see page 45

C h a n n e l

Weston-super-Mare
Steep Holm Island

Bridgwater Bay

AVON

American Costume
Farleigh

Bath

Trowbridge

Mendip Hills

Brokerswood

Longleat

Porlock Minehead Dunster
Cloutsham

Burnham-on-Sea
Watchet
A39
Bridgwater

Cheddar
Wookey Hole

Wells

Nunney
Cranmore

Warminster

WILTSHIRE

Exmoor

Quantock Hills

Shepton Mallet

Rural Life
Glastonbury
Shoes   Street

A361
A37

Stourhead

S O M E R S E T

A361

Taunton

R. Parrett

Yeovilton
Aircraft

A303

Shaftesbury
A30

Bickleigh Mill
Tiverton

A303

Yeovil
Montacute

Sherborne
Compton House

R. Exe

M5

Chard
Crewkerne

D O R S E T

Blandford Forum

Milton Abbas
Farm

A377

Killerton

Cricket St Thomas

Parnham
Beaminster

Cerne Abbas
Dinosaurs

Athelhampton
A35

Exeter

Fossils

Bridport
A35

Dorchester

Bovington Camp

Castle Drogo

Lyme Regis

Maiden Castle

Tanks

A30

Powderham

Sidmouth

Abbotsbury

Lodmoor Country Park

Kimmeridge

Bovey Tracey
Widecombe
A38

Steam and Countryside
Exmouth
Dawlish

Lyme Bay

Chesil Bank

Weymouth
Lulworth Cove

Newton Abbot
Teignmouth

Compton

Portland Bill

Totnes Costume Torquay Torbay Paignton

Dartmouth

Steam Engines

Kingsbridge

N
W — E
S

0 10 20 30 40 Kilometres
0 5 10 15 20 25 Miles

Salcombe
Start Point

Channel Islands

Cherbourg

see page 40

You can go down the caves at **Wookey Hole**. In ancient times people used to live in the caverns.

Wells Cathedral is built in the medieval Gothic style. It has about 300 statues carved on its west front.

At the **Fleet Air Arm Museum**, Yeovilton, you can see the original model of Concorde and sit in the cockpits of naval aircraft.

Montacute House was built in Elizabethan times. Its long gallery is the longest of that age in England.

Torquay became a popular seaside resort in the 1800s. It has such a mild climate that palm trees grow there.

The 150m high cliffs at **Sidmouth** are of old red sandstone. The sand on the beach is red too.

Abbotsbury Swannery is a colony of hundreds of swans. It was probably founded by monks in the 14th century.

In the village of **Milton Abbas** you can see many thatched cottages which are typical of the West Country.

South Wales

see page 46

You can go on a steam train on the **Vale of Rheidol Railway** high up into the hills from Aberystwyth.

This cromlech at **Pentre Ifan** is the remains of a Stone Age burial chamber. "Cromlech" is Welsh for dolmen.

In the **Dan-yr-Ogof Caves** you can see weird rock formations and underground lakes.

Penscynor Wildlife Park has a good bird collection, including many parrots. These are macaws.

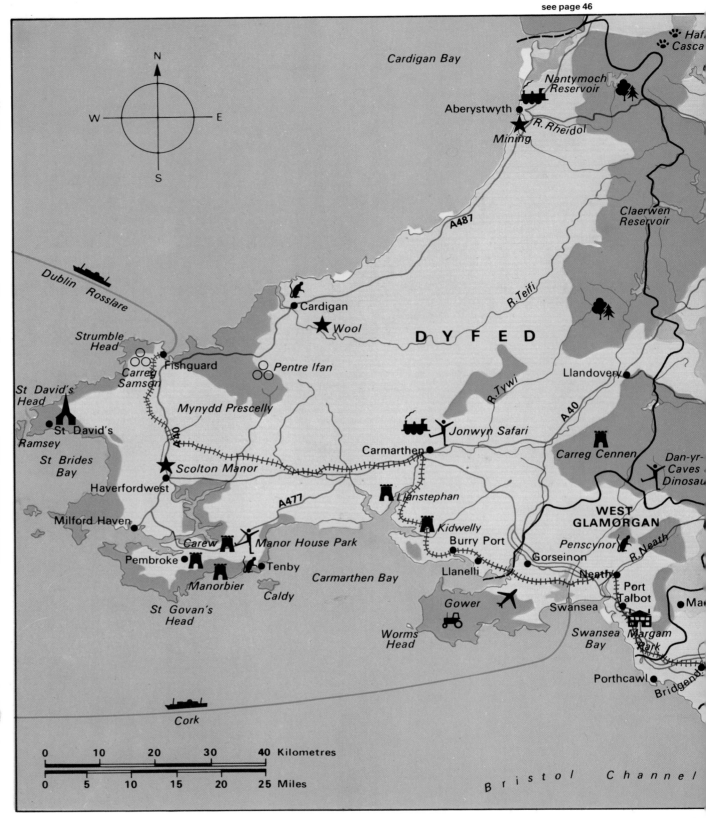

Cardigan Bay

Nantymoch Reservoir

Aberystwyth

Mining

R. Rheidol

Claerwen Reservoir

A487

Dublin
Rosslare

Strumble Head

Cardigan

Wool

R. Teifi

D Y F E D

Fishguard

Pentre Ifan

Carreg Samson

Llandovery

St David's Head

Mynydd Prescelly

R. Tywi

St David's

Ramsey

St Brides Bay

Jonwyn Safari

Scolton Manor

Carmarthen

Carreg Cennen

A40

Dan-yr-
Caves
Dinosau

Haverfordwest

Llanstephan

Milford Haven

A477

Kidwelly

WEST
GLAMORGAN

Carew

Manor House Park

Burry Port

Penscynor

R. Neath

Pembroke

Tenby

Gorseinon

Neath

Manorbier

Carmarthen Bay

Llanelli

Port Talbot

St Govan's Head

Caldy

Gower

Swansea

Ma

Worms Head

Swansea Bay

Margam Park

Porthcawl

Bridgend

Cork

N
W   E
S

0   10   20   30   40 Kilometres

0   5   10   15   20   25 Miles

Bristol Channel

St David's Cathedral is named after Wales's patron saint and St David's is the smallest cathedral city in Britain.

Pembroke Castle is built over a cavern. Its high, round keep has a roof and the gatehouse has three portcullises.

The **Brecon Beacons** got their name because signal fires used to be lit on them. From the top you can see the Bristol Channel.

Caerphilly Castle is the biggest in Wales. One tower was blasted in the 1600s and has been leaning sideways ever since.

see page 47

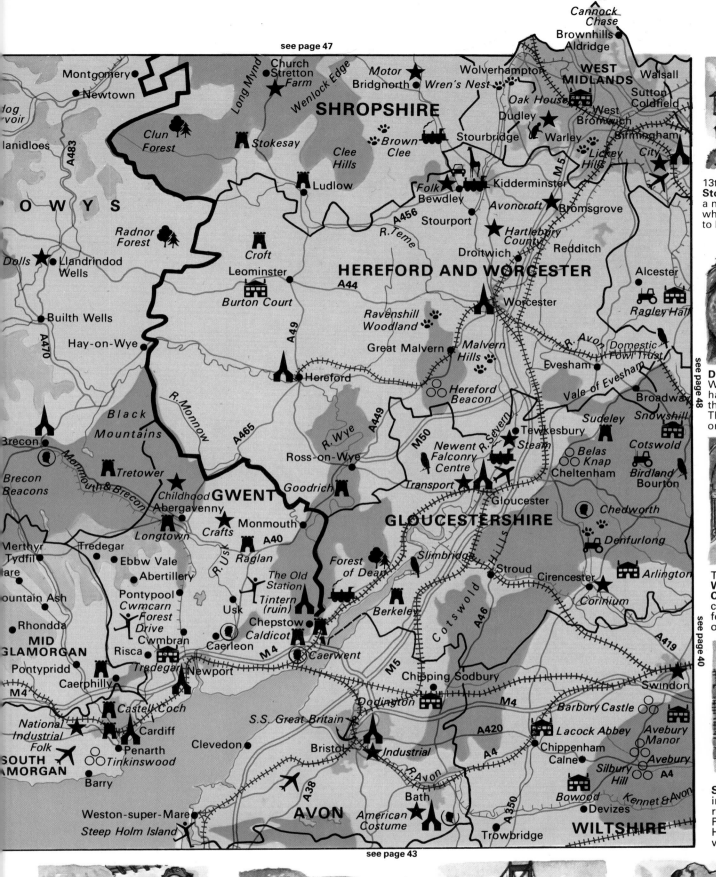

Montgomery
Newton
Clun Forest
Church Stretton
Motor Farm
Wren's Nest
Wolverhampton
WEST MIDLANDS
Walsall
Brownhills
Aldridge
Cannock Chase
Sutton Coldfield
Bridgnorth
SHROPSHIRE
Long Mynd
Wenlock Edge
Oak House
Dudley
West Bromwich
Stokesay
Clee Hills
Brown Clee
Stourbridge
Warley
Lickey Hills
Birmingham City
Ludlow
Folk
Bewdley
Kidderminster
Radnor Forest
Stourport
Avoncroft
Bromsgrove
Dolls
Llandrindod Wells
Croft
Hartlebury County
Droitwich
Redditch
Leominster
HEREFORD AND WORCESTER
Alcester
Builth Wells
Burton Court
Worcester
Ragley Hall
Hay-on-Wye
Ravenshill Woodland
R. Avon
Domestic Fowl Trust
Great Malvern
Malvern Hills
Evesham
Vale of Evesham
Broadway
Snowshill
Hereford
Hereford Beacon
Sudeley
Black Mountains
R. Monnow
Tewkesbury
Steam
Belas Knap
Cotswold
Brecon
Ross-on-Wye
Newent Falconry Centre
Cheltenham
Birdland
Bourton
Brecon Beacons
Tretower
Goodrich
GLOUCESTERSHIRE
Transport
Gloucester
Chedworth
Childhood
Abergavenny
Monmouth
Crafts
GWENT
Denfurlong
Longtown
Raglan
Forest of Dean
Slimbridge
Stroud
Cirencester
Arlington
Merthyr Tydfil
Tredegar
Ebbw Vale
Abertillery
The Old Station
Tintern (ruin)
Usk
Berkeley
Corinium
Cotswold Hills
Mountain Ash
Pontypool
Cwmcarn Forest Drive
Cwmbran
Chepstow
Caldicot
Rhondda
MID GLAMORGAN
Risca
Caerleon
Caerwent
Chipping Sodbury
Swindon
Pontypridd
Tredegar
Newport
Barbury Castle
Caerphilly
Dodington
Lacock Abbey
Avebury Manor
Castell Coch
S.S. Great Britain
Chippenham
Calne
Avebury
National Industrial Folk
Cardiff
Clevedon
Bristol
Industrial
Silbury Hill
SOUTH GLAMORGAN
Penarth
Tinkinswood
American Costume
Bath
Bowood
Devizes
Barry
Weston-super-Mare
Steep Holm Island
Trowbridge
WILTSHIRE
POWYS
A483
A470
A465
A40
A449
A44
A456
A49
A46
A4
A420
A419
A38
A350
M5
M4
M50
R. Teme
R. Wye
R. Usk
R. Severn
R. Avon
Kennet & Avon

see page 48
see page 40
see page 43

13th century **Stokesay Castle** is a manor house which was fortified to keep out raiders.

Dudley Zoo, in the West Midlands, has over a thousand animals. This is an orang-utan.

The oldest part of **Worcester Cathedral** is the crypt, built in 1084 for the safekeeping of saints' relics.

Sudeley Castle has interesting Tudor relics. Catherine Parr, the last of Henry VIII's six wives, lived here.

The **Welsh Folk Museum** in Cardiff has old buildings from all over Wales, including cottages, farms, a chapel and a mill.

Tintern Abbey is one of the monasteries destroyed by Henry VIII when he broke away from the Catholic Church in 1536.

The M4 motorway from England to Wales crosses the River Severn by the kilometre-long **Severn Suspension Bridge**.

Avebury Henge was built about the same time as Stonehenge. Avebury village is inside the stone circles.

45

North Wales

At **Llandudno** you can go on Britain's longest cable-hauled tramway to the top of the Great Orme headland.

Edward I built **Conwy Castle** as a stronghold against the Welsh after defeating Prince Llywelyn.

This stone passage leads to the burial chamber of the prehistoric mound or "cairn" of **Bryn Celli Du.**

The **Museum of Childhood** at Beaumaris has toys and games from the last 150 years. This is a clockwork cat.

0   10   20   30   40 Kilometres

0 5 10 15 20 25 Miles

N
W   E
S

Irish Sea

Isle of Man

Isle of Man

Dublin

Dublin

Carmel Head

Amlwch

Din Lligwy

Great Ormes Head

Doll & Railway

Llandudno

Rhyl

Holyhead

Caer Gybi

Anglesey

Colwyn Bay

Rhudd

Holy Is.

Llangefni

Beaumaris

Conwy

Welsh Mountain

Plas Newydd

Bangor

Penrhyn Castle

Denbigh

Bryn Celli Ddu

Childhood

Llanrwst

Hendrai

Gwydir

C L W

Menai Strait

Caernarfon

Quarrying

Llanberis

Dolbardarn

Caernarfon Bay

▲ Snowdon

R. Conwy

Snowdonia

Beddgelert

Gloddfa Ganol Mountain Centre

Blaenau-Ffestiniog

Slate Caverns

A470

A494

Criccieth

Porthmadog

Ffestiniog

G W Y N E D D

Pwllheli

Llyn Trawsfynydd

Lleyn

Tremadog Bay

Harlech

L. Bala

Cefn Isa Farm

Dolgefeiliau

L. Vyrnwy

Penkilan Head

Dolgellau

Bardsey

Barmouth

A458

Cader Idris

A487

P O W Y S

Tywyn

Machynlleth

Cardigan Bay

Hafren Cascades

Mo

see page 44

Caernarfon Castle is one of eight castles Edward I built in Wales in the 1200s when he was trying to conquer the country.

Snowdon is the highest mountain in England and Wales (1085m). You can sometimes see as far as Ireland from the top.

At **Gloddfa Ganol** you can go down an old mine and learn about the history of the slate mining industry in Wales.

Harlech Castle was built on a good defensive site – on a high crag by the sea, with mountains behind. It also has a moat.

see page 53

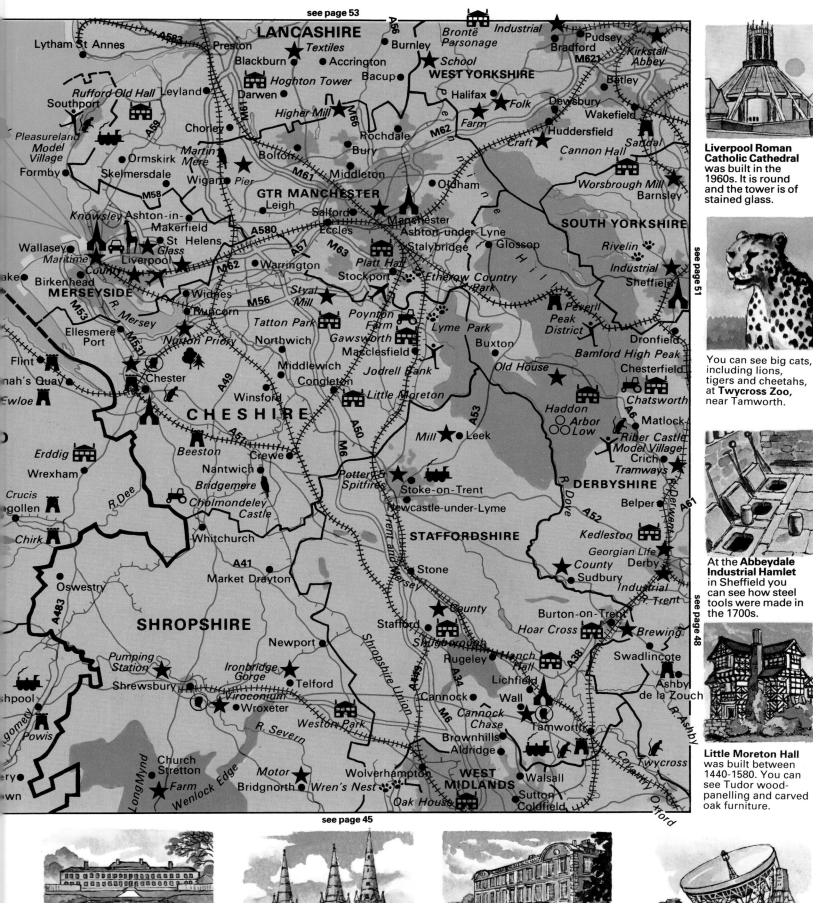

LANCASHIRE

Lytham St Annes
Preston
Blackburn
Burnley
Accrington
Bacup
Textiles
Brontë Parsonage
Industrial
Pudsey
Bradford
Kirkstall Abbey
School
WEST YORKSHIRE
Batley
Rufford Old Hall
Leyland
Darwen
Hoghton Tower
Halifax
Folk Farm
Dewsbury
Wakefield
Sandal
Southport
Higher Mill
Rochdale
Huddersfield
Craft
Cannon Hall
Chorley
Bury
Martin Mere
Bolton
Middleton
Oldham
Worsbrough Mill
Barnsley
Ormskirk
Pleasureland Model Village
Formby
Skelmersdale
Wigan *Pier*
GTR MANCHESTER
Leigh
Salford
Eccles
Manchester
Ashton-under-Lyne
Stalybridge
Glossop
SOUTH YORKSHIRE
Rivelin
Industrial
Sheffield
Knowsley
Ashton-in-Makerfield
St Helens *Glass*
Wallasey
Maritime
County
Liverpool
Warrington
Platt Hall
Stockport
Etherow Country Park
Birkenhead
MERSEYSIDE
Widnes
Runcorn
Styal Mill
Poynton Farm
Lyme Park
Dronfield
Peak District
Peveril
Bamford High Peak
Chesterfield
Ellesmere Port
Flint
Norton Priory
Tatton Park
Northwich
Gawsworth
Macclesfield
Buxton
Old House
Chatsworth
Matlock
Chester
Middlewich
Congleton
Jodrell Bank
Little Moreton
Haddon
Arbor Low
Riber Castle Model Village
Crich *Tramways*
CHESHIRE
Winsford
Beeston
Crewe
Nantwich
Mill Leek
Haddon
DERBYSHIRE
Belper
Erddig
Wrexham
Bridgemere
Cholmondeley Castle
Pottery Spitfires
Stoke-on-Trent
Newcastle-under-Lyme
Kedleston
Georgian Life
Derby
Crucis
Whitchurch
STAFFORDSHIRE
County
Sudbury
Industrial
Chirk
Oswestry
Market Drayton
Stone
Burton-on-Trent
Brewing
Swadlincote
SHROPSHIRE
Newport
County
Stafford
Shugborough
Hoar Cross
Ashby de la Zouch
Powis
Pumping Station
Ironbridge Gorge
Telford
Rugeley
Hanch Hall
Shrewsbury
Viroconium
Wroxeter
Weston Park
Cannock
Cannock Chase
Lichfield
Wall
Tamworth
Church Stretton
Farm
Motor
Bridgnorth
Wren's Nest
Wolverhampton
WEST MIDLANDS
Walsall
Sutton Coldfield
Twycross
Wenlock Edge
Oak House
Brownhills
Aldridge

see page 51
see page 48
see page 45

Liverpool Roman Catholic Cathedral was built in the 1960s. It is round and the tower is of stained glass.

You can see big cats, including lions, tigers and cheetahs, at **Twycross Zoo**, near Tamworth.

At the **Abbeydale Industrial Hamlet** in Sheffield you can see how steel tools were made in the 1700s.

Little Moreton Hall was built between 1440-1580. You can see Tudor wood-panelling and carved oak furniture.

At **Erddig Hall** you can see the servants' rooms as well as the master's, and also a laundry, bakehouse, sawmill and smithy.

Lichfield Cathedral is the only English cathedral which has three spires. They are known as the Ladies of the Vale.

There are woodland walks and a woodland adventure playground in the big parklands of 17th century **Weston Park**.

Jodrell Bank has a big radio telescope which studies objects in space. There is also a small telescope to look through.

Eastern England

You can see the world's largest collection of single-seater racing cars in the **Donington Collection**.

Belvoir Castle was rebuilt in the 1800s to look like a medieval castle. Jousts are often held there.

You can learn about the history of brewing at the **Bass Museum of Brewing**. There is a model of a Victorian brewery.

Coventry Cathedral was bombed in World War II and its ruins are now joined to a modern cathedral.

see page 51
see page 47
see page 45
see page 40

This plasterwork room is in 17th century **Ragley Hall**. There is an adventure wood and a woodland walk in the grounds.

Today the **Grand Union Canal** is used for pleasure, but the narrow boats used to transport heavy industrial goods.

There are many Tudor houses in **Warwickshire**. Some are small and thatched, and some are large like the one shown above.

There are good views from **Rockingham Castle**, which is built on top of a hill. You can see five counties.

The Wash

Brancaster

• Hunstanton

Warham Camp

NORFOLK

Houghton

⚔ Castle Rising

Great Witchingham   Blickling

Sutton Windmill   The Broads

Cromer

R. Bure

★ Social History • King's Lynn

Great Ouse

Wisbech

A17

★ Rural Life
East Dereham

Ferry

• Downham Market

• Swaffham

Mustard

Norwich ★
Craft

A47   Caister
★ Maritime
Great Yarmouth
Burgh Castle

Somerleyton

• March

The Fens

Oxburgh

A1065

Grimes Graves

Little Ouse

Banham

Lowestoft

Ely

Kilverstone

• Thetford

A11

A143

Otter Trust

Kessingland

Southwold

Clocks

Framlingham

R. Waveney

SUFFOLK

Aldeburgh

Newmarket
Anglesey
William
Cambridge
Colleges

Ickworth

A134

• Bury St Edmunds

Stowmarket

Helmingham Hall

★ Rural Life

R. Orwell

Orford

Orford Ness

Aircraft

Linton

Clocks

Lavenham   R. Stour

Guildhall

Sudbury
Gainsborough

Christchurch

Ipswich

Esbjerg

MT11

A130

Audley End

• Saffron Walden

R. Colne

Natural History

Heavy Horses

Felixstowe

Bremerhaven

Harwich

Hook of Holland

ESSEX

Widdington

A604   Curios

Castle Museum
Colchester

Stansted
Braintree   Gosfield

Frinton

Brightlingsea

• Clacton-on-Sea

Stortford

R. Lea   R. Roding

A414
Harlow

A12

Chelmsford   R. Blackwater

| 0 | 10 | 20 | 30 | 40 Kilometres |

| 0 | 5 | 10 | 15 | 20 | 25 Miles |

see page 41

The **North Norfolk Railway** has historic engines and carriages. You can sometimes go on a steam train.

The **Norfolk Broads** were peat workings which flooded and became lakes. Now you can go sailing on them.

At **Grimes Graves** you can see the remains of a prehistoric flint mine which is 4,000 years old.

Ely Cathedral stands out above the flat landscape of the Fens. It has an unusual, eight-sided tower.

The deer park at **Woburn Abbey** has nine species of deer. Some, like this Père David's, are extinct in the wild.

Audley End was begun in 1605, but many rooms inside are the work of the famous 18th century designer, Robert Adam.

The **Museum of East Anglian Life** at Stowmarket has farm tools, carts and old country buildings.

You can see prehistoric and Roman relics in **Colchester Castle Museum,** which is in the keep of the Norman Castle.

49

North-East England

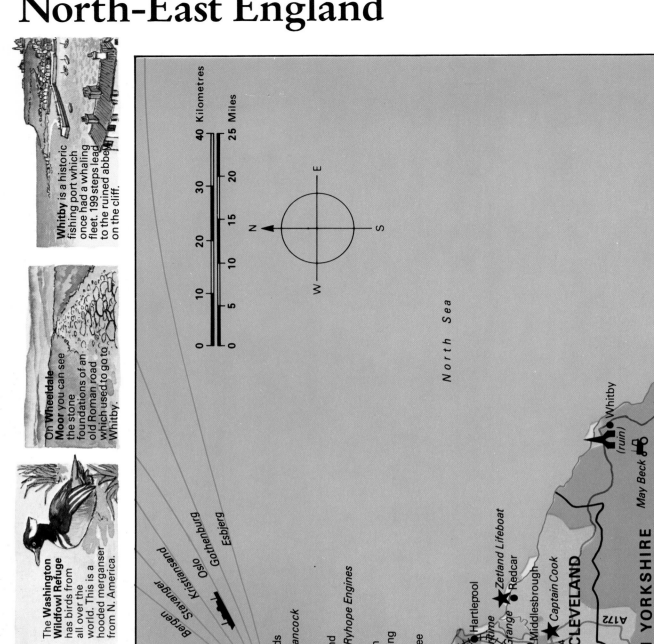

North Sea

40 Kilometres
25 Miles

Esbjerg
Gothenburg
Oslo
Kristiansand
Stavanger
Bergen

NORTHUMBERLAND

Ashington
Morpeth
Blyth
St Mary's Island
Whitley Bay
Tynemouth
South Shields
Science, Antiquities, Hancock
Christianity
Fort
Seaton Delaval
Gateshead
Washington
Stanley
Open Air

TYNE & WEAR

Newcastle
Old Hall Station, Ryhope Engines
Sunderland
Houghton-le-Spring
Seaham
Chester-le-Street
Peterlee

DURHAM

Durham
Bishop Auckland
Witton
Darlington
Richmond

Hartlepool
Zetland Lifeboat
Redcar
Maritime
Middlesbrough
Newham Grange
Captain Cook

CLEVELAND

Preston Hall
Stockton-on-Tees
Teesside
Railway

NORTH YORKSHIRE

Whitby *(ruin)*
May Beck
Wheeldale Moor
North York Moors
Forestry Commission
Peasholm Park
Scarborough
Flamingoland
Rural Life
Pickering
Helmsley
Ryedale Folk
Rievaulx *(ruin)*
Byland *(ruin)*
Mount Grace *(ruin)*
R. Derwent
A171
A170
A165

R. Swale
R. Ure
A1
A684
A19
A172
A174
A689
A690
A66
A68
A1(M)

Lightwater Valley
Ripon

see page 52

see page 53

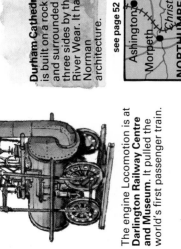

Whitby is a historic fishing port which once had a whaling fleet. 199 steps lead to the ruined abbey on the cliff.

On **Wheeldale Moor** you can see the stone foundations of an old Roman road which used to go to Whitby.

The **Washington Wildfowl Refuge** has birds from all over the world. This is a hooded merganser from N. America.

Durham Cathedral is built on a rock and surrounded on three sides by the River Wear. It has Norman architecture.

The engine Locomotion is at **Darlington Railway Centre and Museum**. It pulled the world's first passenger train.

The **Lightwater Valley Theme Park** has many rides and amusements, including a fortress playground.

The monks at **Fountains Abbey** traded in wool. It became one of the richest monasteries in Europe in the Middle Ages.

Castle Howard is a great house built in the 18th century in the classical style. There is a collection of historic costumes.

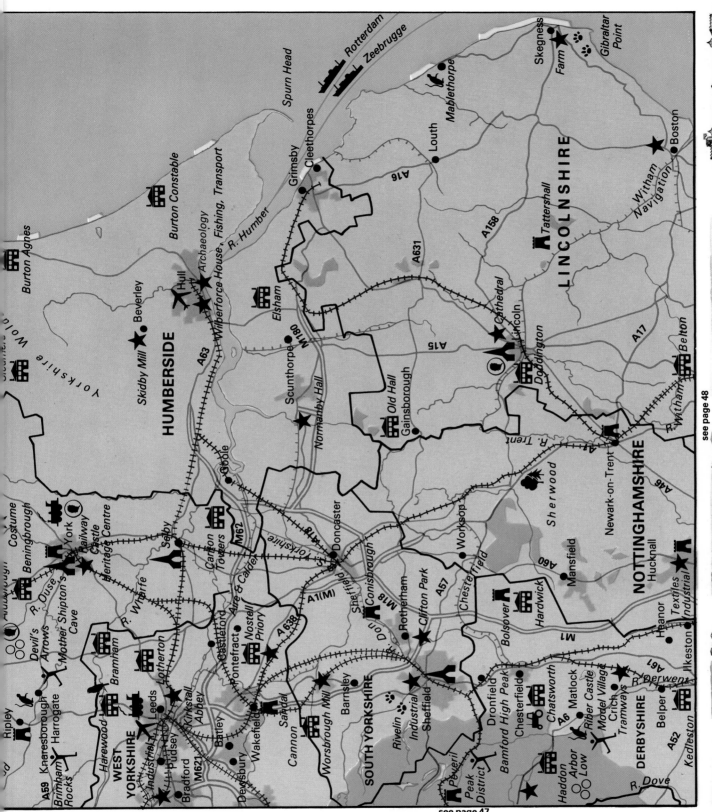

HUMBERSIDE

Yorkshire Wolds

Burton Agnes

Skidby Mill • Beverley
Hull ★ Archaeology
Wilberforce House, Fishing, Transport
R. Humber
Burton Constable

Rotterdam
Zeebrugge
Spurn Head
Grimsby
Cleethorpes
Elsham
M180
A63
Scunthorpe
Normanby Hall
Goole

A16
Louth
Mablethorpe
Skegness ★
Farm
Boston ★
Gibraltar Point
Witham Navigation

LINCOLNSHIRE
A631
A158
Cathedral ★ Lincoln
Doddington
Gainsborough
Old Hall
A15
R. Trent
A1
Newark-on-Trent
Sherwood
Worksop
A46
A17
Belton
R. Witham
Tattershall ▲

NOTTINGHAMSHIRE
Mansfield
A60
Hucknall ▲
Textiles (Industrial)
Heanor
Ilkeston
M1
Bolsover
Hardwick ▲
Chesterfield
Clifton Park
Rotherham
Conisbrough
Doncaster
A1(M)
Sheffield
St. Yorkshire
A638
Selby
Carlton Towers
M62

SOUTH YORKSHIRE
Barnsley
Worsbrough Mill
Wakefield
Sandal
Cannon
Industrial Sheffield
Rivelin
Dronfield
Chesterfield
Chatsworth
Matlock A6
Riber Castle
Crich Model Village
Tramways
R. Derwent
A61
Belper
Kedleston A52
DERBYSHIRE
Haddon
Arbor Low
Bamford High Peak
Peak District ▲
Peveril
R. Dove

WEST YORKSHIRE
Leeds
Kirkstall Abbey
Pudsey
Bradford M621
Dewsbury
Batley
Industrial
Pontefract
Nostell Priory
Castleford
Lotherton
Bramham
Harewood
Aire & Calder
R. Calder

York
Railway
Castle
Heritage Centre
Beningbrough
R. Ouse
Mother Shipton's Cave
Devil's Arrows
Ripley
Knaresborough
Harrogate
A59
Brimham Rocks
Costume
R. Wharfe
R. Aire
Don
M18

see page 47

see page 48

At **Burton Constable** there is a science museum and a collection of carriages.

Lincoln Cathedral is the third largest cathedral in Britain, after St Paul's and York Minster.

In **Chatsworth Farmyard** you can see animals from close to, watch cows being milked and horses shod.

Conisbrough Castle has one of the oldest round keeps in England. It was built in about 1185.

The **Devil's Arrows** are three huge monoliths from prehistoric times. Legend says the devil shot them at a local city.

York Minster is a cathedral but has kept the Anglo-Saxon name for a large church. It has over 100 stained glass windows.

There are exotic, endangered and wild birds at **Harewood Bird Garden**. This is a Victoria crowned pigeon.

In the **Abbey House Museum**, Kirkstall, there are Georgian and Victorian streets, rebuilt as they used to be.
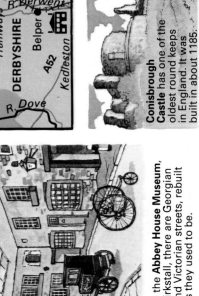

Northern England

see page 50

see page 57

Statues stand on top of the huge barbican at **Alnwick Castle**. You can visit the keep, armoury and dungeon.

The **Farne Islands** are a nature reserve for seals and many different seabirds, including guillemots.

At **Gladstone Court Museum** in Biggar you can see a 19th century street with shops, a bank and a library.

Jedburgh Abbey has Norman architecture. It fell into ruins after the English burnt it during wars against the Scots.

Map labels

North Sea

Science, Antiquities *Hancock*
Old Hall

Berwick-on-Tweed
Eyemouth
Holy Island
Lindisfarne
Farne Islands
Bamburgh
Belford
Chillingham Castle
Dunstanburgh
Warkworth
Alnwick
Newbiggin-by-the-Sea
Blyth
Ashington
Morpeth
Bagpipe
Seaton Delaval
Christianity
TYNE & WEAR
Newcastle
Gateshead
Washington
Chester-le-Street
Open Air
Stanley
Consett

Heatherslaw Mill
A697
A691
Glanton
Wooler
Cragside
Wallington
A696
A68
R. Coquet
NORTHUMBERLAND
Chesters
Corbridge
R. Tyne
Hexham
Carrawburgh
Housesteads
Chesterholm
Hadrian's Wall
Tractor & Farm Machinery
R. Tyne

R. Tweed
A1
A68
Manderston
Duns
Floors
Kelso
Dryburgh (ruin)
Smailholm
Melrose
(ruin)
Jedburgh
Jail
BORDERS
Lauder
Galashiels
Abbotsford
Selkirk
Old Ironmongery
Textiles
R. Teviot
Hawick
Hermitage
Cheviot Hills
Border Forest Park
Kielder Water
Birdoswald
Carlisle
CUMBRIA
R. Eden
R. Esk

A7
Moorfoot Hills
Peebles
Innerleithen
Traquair House
Neidpath
Penicuik
A72
A702
A7
Bowhill
Tweedsmuir Hills
Langholm
Lockerbie
Burnswark
DUMFRIES & GALLOWAY
Rammerscales
Annan
R. Annan
Moffat
A74
A75
A701
A76
STRATHCLYDE
Shops
Biggar
Lanark
A702
Ae Forest
Burns' House
Windmill
Dumfries
Caerlaverock
Sweetheart (ruin)
Solway Firth
A596

see page 55

Corbridge used to be a Roman town. This sculpture of a lion attacking another animal is in **Corbridge Roman Museum.**

Raby Castle has a great hall big enough to hold 6 small houses. You can also see the medieval kitchen and servants' hall.

Scafell Pike, in the Lake District, is England's highest mountain (977m). You can see several lakes from the top.

Windermere is the biggest lake in England. It is more than 16km long and you can go for steamer and boat trips on it.

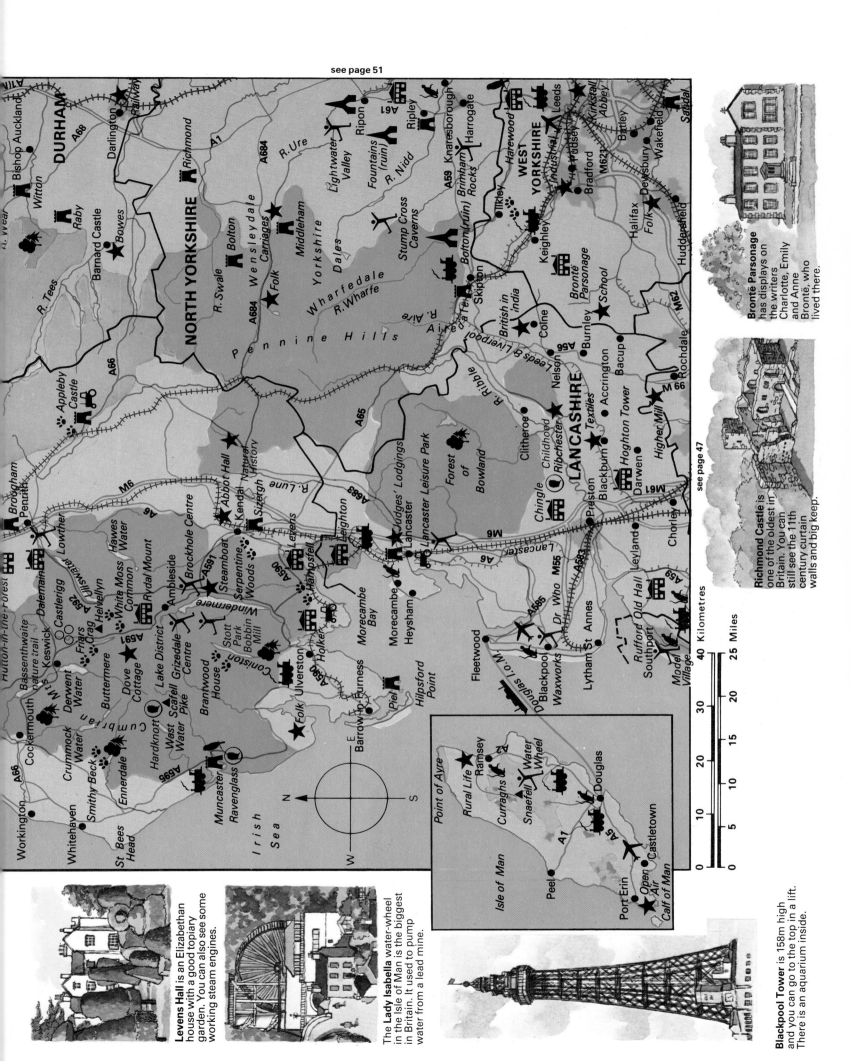

see page 51

Brontë Parsonage has displays on the writers Charlotte, Emily and Anne Brontë, who lived there.

Richmond Castle is one of the oldest in Britain. You can still see the 11th century curtain walls and big keep.

see page 47

Levens Hall is an Elizabethan house with a good topiary garden. You can also see some working steam engines.

The **Lady Isabella** water-wheel in the Isle of Man is the biggest in Britain. It used to pump water from a lead mine.

Blackpool Tower is 158m high and you can go to the top in a lift. There is an aquarium inside.

South-West Scotland

see page 57

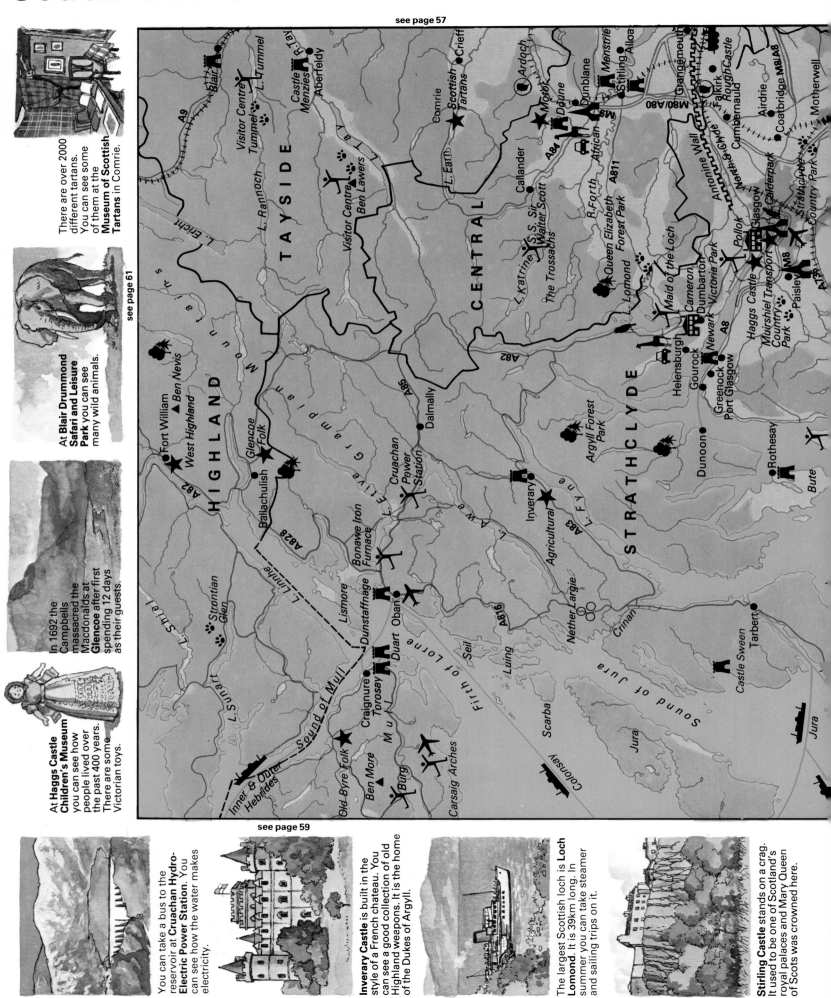

There are over 2000 different tartans. You can see some of them at the **Museum of Scottish Tartans** in Comrie.

see page 61

At **Blair Drummond Safari and Leisure Park** you can see many wild animals.

In 1692 the Campbells massacred the Macdonalds at **Glencoe** after first spending 12 days as their guests.

At **Haggs Castle Children's Museum** you can see how people lived over the past 400 years. There are some Victorian toys.

see page 59

You can take a bus to the reservoir at **Cruachan Hydro-Electric Power Station**. You can see how the water makes electricity.

Inverary Castle is built in the style of a French chateau. You can see a good collection of old Highland weapons. It is the home of the Dukes of Argyll.

The largest Scottish loch is **Loch Lomond**. It is 39km long. In summer you can take steamer and sailing trips on it.

Stirling Castle stands on a crag. It used to be one of Scotland's royal palaces and Mary Queen of Scots was crowned here.

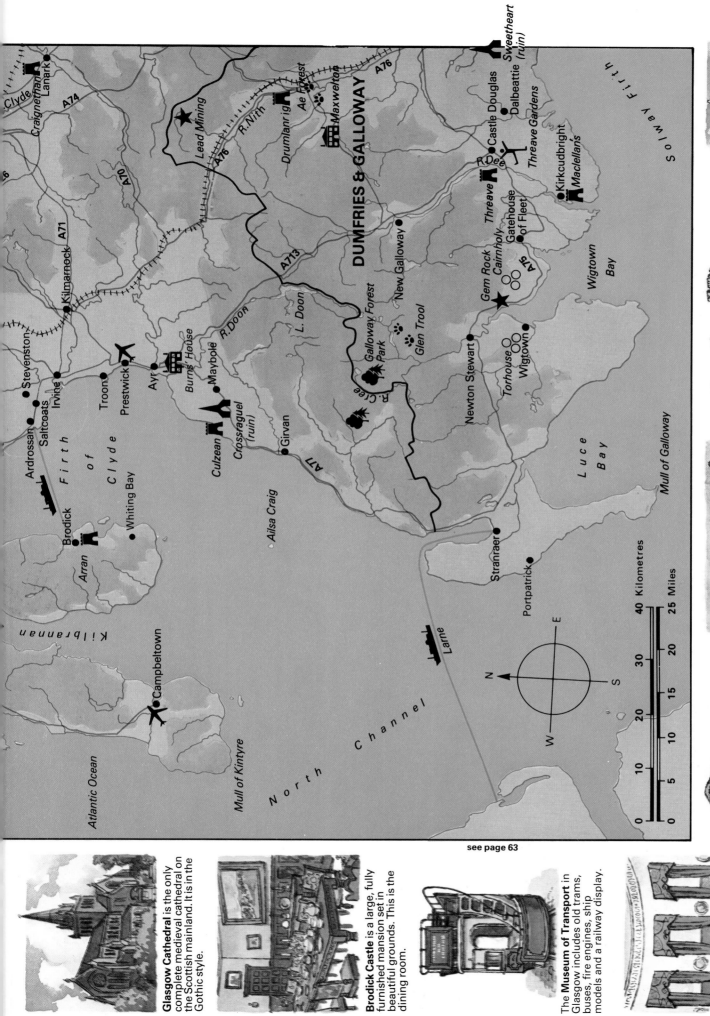

see page 63

Lady Devorgilla founded **Sweetheart Abbey** in memory of her husband. Both are buried there.

You can still see the gallows knob on **Threave Castle** where Archibald the Grim used to hang his enemies.

At **Cairnholy** you can see two chambered burial mounds or "cairns" from prehistoric times.

Burns' House was the childhood home of Robert Burns, poet and writer of "Auld Lang Syne". It is now a museum.

Glasgow Cathedral is the only complete medieval cathedral on the Scottish mainland. It is in the Gothic style.

Brodick Castle is a large, fully furnished mansion set in beautiful grounds. This is the dining room.

The **Museum of Transport** in Glasgow includes old trams, buses, fire engines, ship models and a railway display.

This is the round drawing room at **Culzean Castle**, which was designed by Robert Adam in the elegant 18th century style.

Eastern Scotland

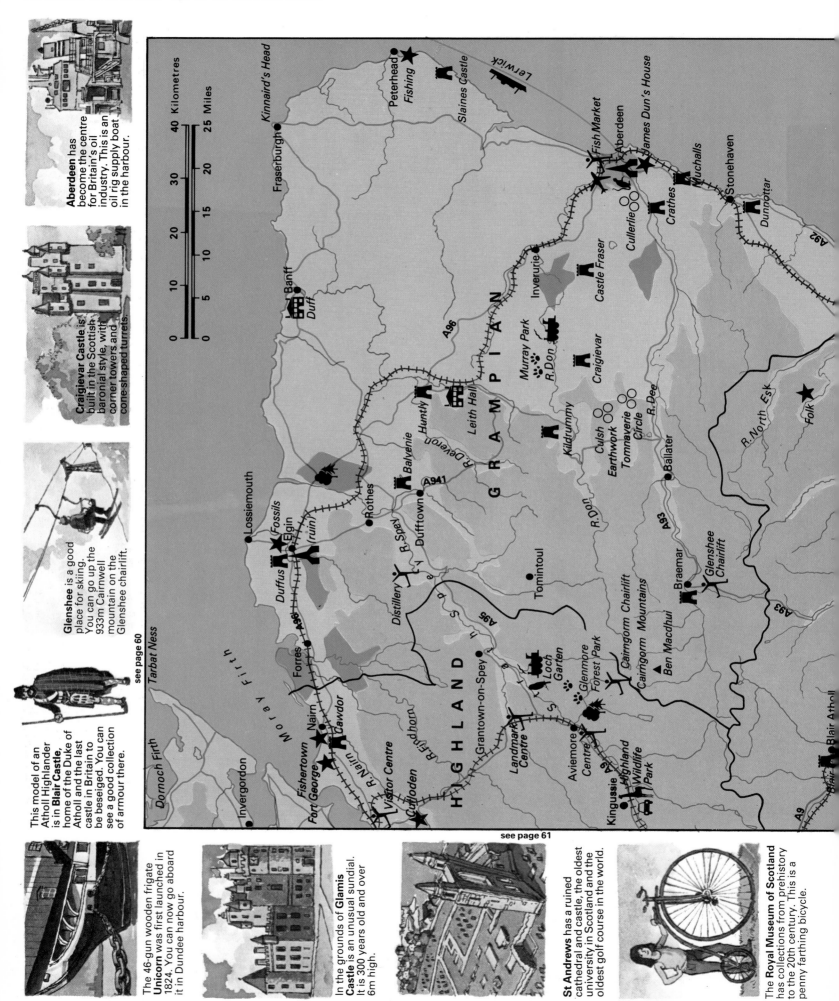

Aberdeen has become the centre for Britain's oil industry. This is an oil rig supply boat in the harbour.

Craigievar Castle is built in the Scottish baronial style, with corner towers and cone-shaped turrets.

Glenshee is a good place for skiing. You can go up the 933m Cairnwell mountain on the Glenshee chairlift.

This model of an Atholl Highlander is in **Blair Castle**, home of the Duke of Atholl and the last castle in Britain to be besieged. You can see a good collection of armour there.

The 46-gun wooden frigate **Unicorn** was first launched in 1824. You can now go aboard it in Dundee harbour.

In the grounds of **Glamis Castle** is an unusual sundial. It is 300 years old and over 6m high.

St Andrews has a ruined cathedral and castle, the oldest university in Scotland and the oldest golf course in the world.

The **Royal Museum of Scotland** has collections from prehistory to the 20th century. This is a penny farthing bicycle.

see page 60

see page 61

Map labels:
Kinnaird's Head, Lerwick, Peterhead, Fishing, Slaines Castle, James Dun's House, Aberdeen, Fish Market, Muchalls, Stonehaven, Dunnottar, Fraserburgh, Crathes, Cullerlie, Castle Fraser, Inverurie, A96, Murray Park, R. Don, Craigievar, Banff, Duff, Kildrummy, Culsh Earthwork, Tomnaverie Circle, R. Dee, Ballater, Folk, R. North Esk, Leith Hall, Huntly, R. Deveron, GRAMPIAN, Balvenie, A941, Rothes, Dufftown, R. Spey, Lossiemouth, Fossils, Elgin (ruin), Tomintoul, A93, Braemar, Glenshee Chairlift, Duffus, Distillery, A95, Cairngorm Chairlift, Glenmore Forest Park, Cairngorm Mountains, Ben Macdhui, A93, Forres, Loch Garten, Tarbat Ness, HIGHLAND, Grantown-on-Spey, R. Findhorn, Moray Firth, Nairn, Cawdor, Landmark Centre, Aviemore Centre, Highland Wildlife Park, Dornoch Firth, Invergordon, Fort George, Fishertown, R. Nairn, Culloden, Visitor Centre, Kingussie, Blair Atholl, A9

25 Miles
40 Kilometres
30   20
20   15
10   10
5
0   0

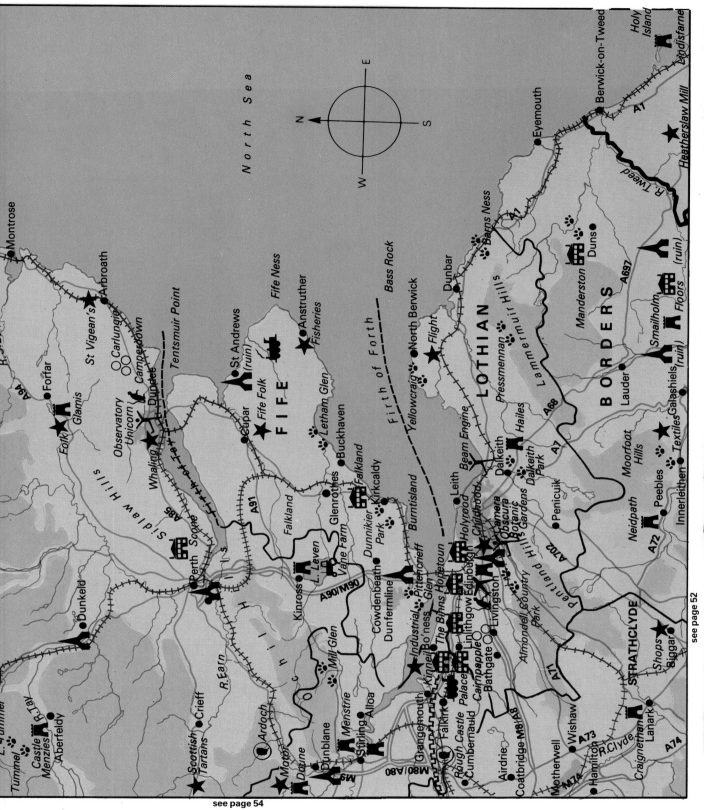

see page 54

see page 52

You can go on a boat trip round **Bass Rock.** Its population of seabirds includes 8,000 gannets.

Mary Queen of Scots lived at the **Palace of Holyroodhouse.** You can see the state apartments.

The Romans built the turf rampart and ditch of the Antonine Wall. You can see remains at **Rough Castle.**

You can see old railway vehicles at the **Scottish Railway Preservation Society,** Bo'ness.

This is the king's bedchamber in 16th century **Falkland Palace.** The Stewart monarchs liked to go to Falkland to hunt.

The **Forth Road Bridge** was opened in 1964. At 1006m it is Britain's second longest suspension bridge.

You can see exotic plants from all over the world at **Edinburgh Royal Botanic Gardens.** These are giant lilies.

Hopetoun House is an 18th century Adam mansion in large parklands. There is a nature trail and a rooftop viewpoint.

North-West Scotland

see page 60

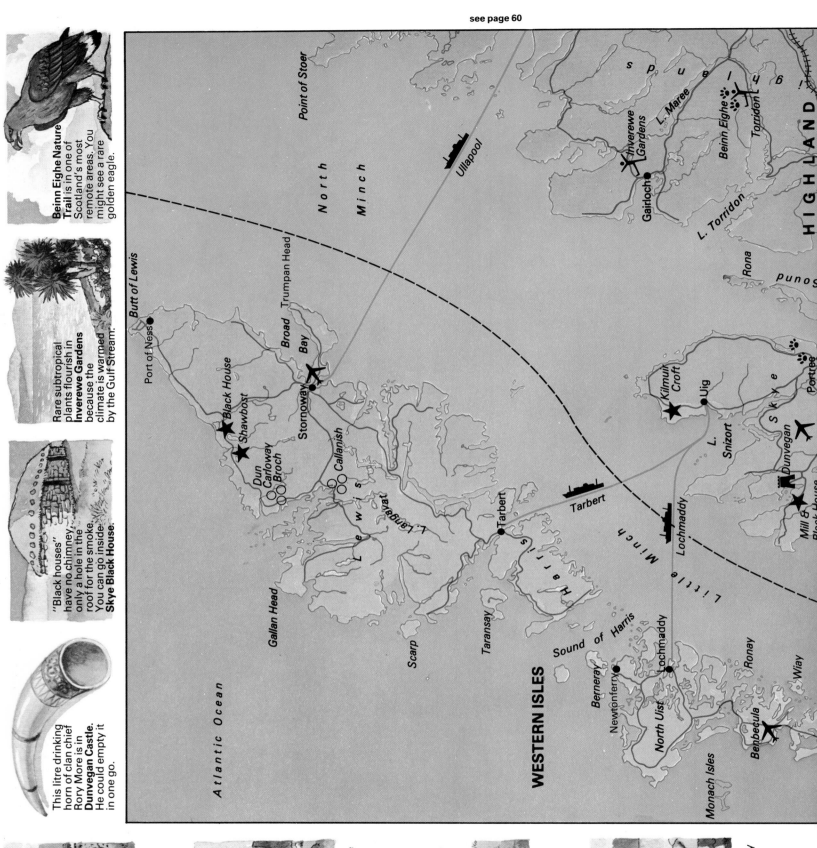

HIGHLAND

Spue lub
L. Maree
Inverewe Gardens
Beinn Eighe
Torridon
Gairloch
L. Torridon
Rona
Sound
North Minch
Ullapool
Point of Stoer

Butt of Lewis
Port of Ness
Broad Bay
Trumpan Head
Black House
Shawbost
Dun Carloway Broch
Stornoway
Callanish
L. Langavat
Lewis
Gallan Head
Scarp
Taransay
Harris
Tarbert
Sound of Harris
Little Minch

Skye
Kilmuir Croft
Uig
L. Snizort
Dunvegan
Portree
Mill &
Black House

Lochmaddy
Bernera
Newtonferry
North Uist
Lochmaddy
Ronay
Wiay
Benbecula
Monach Isles

WESTERN ISLES

Atlantic Ocean

Beinn Eighe Nature Trail is in one of Scotland's most remote areas. You might see a rare golden eagle.

Rare subtropical plants flourish in **Inverewe Gardens** because the climate is warmed by the Gulf Stream.

"Black houses" have no chimney, only a hole in the roof for the smoke. You can go inside **Skye Black House.**

This litre drinking horn of clan chief Rory More is in **Dunvegan Castle.** He could empty it in one go.

Stornoway is the main town in the Western Isles. The Vikings launched attacks from its harbour in the 11th century.

There is a legend that the Bronze Age **Callanish Standing Stones** are a circle of petrified giants.

The **Skye Museum of Crofting Life** is at Kilmuir. You can see Highland furniture and household and farming tools.

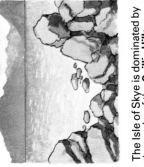

The Isle of Skye is dominated by the peaks of the **Cuillin Hills.** The area is good for climbing.

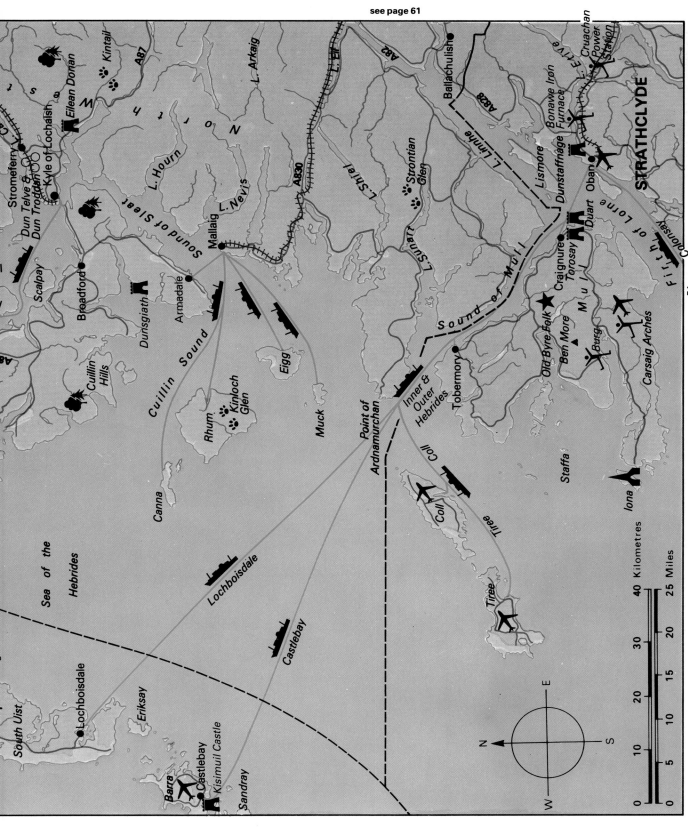

STRATHCLYDE

see page 54

Kintail

Eilean Donan

A87

L. Arkaig

L. Eil

A82

Ballachulish

Stromeferry

Kyle of Lochalsh

Dun Telve &
Dun Troddan

Scalpay

L. Hourn

North

L. Nevis

Sound of Sleat

A830

L. Shiel

Strontian
Glen

A861

Bonawe Iron
Furnace

L. Etive

Cruachan
Power
Station

Lismore

L. Linnhe

Dunstaffnage

Oban

Duart

Broadford

Cuillin
Hills

Dunsgiath

Armadale

Cuillin Sound

Eigg

Kinloch
Glen

Rhum

Muck

Point of
Ardnamurchan

Inner &
Outer
Hebrides

Tobermory

Sound of Mull

L. Sunart

Craignure

Torosay

Old Byre Folk

Ben More

Burg

Mull

Carsaig Arches

Firth of Lorne

Colonsay

Canna

Sea of the
Hebrides

Coll

Coll

Staffa

Iona

Tiree

Tiree

Lochboisdale

Castlebay

South Uist

L. Druidibeg

Lochboisdale

Eriksay

Sandray

Barra

Castlebay

Kisimuil Castle

40 Kilometres

25 Miles

0 5 10 15 20 25

0 10 20 30 40

N
W — E
S

The most usual way of getting to the Scottish islands is by boat. This is the ferry Islands of the West.

In **Duart Castle** dungeon you can see models of prisoners from a Spanish galleon which was blown up in 1588.

Loch Druidibeg nature reserve is the most important breeding ground in Britain for greylag geese.

The owners of **Kisimuil Castle** were well-known for piracy and used to seize English ships.

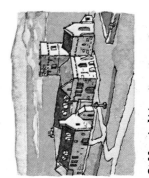

Eilean Donan Castle was built where three lochs meet. In 1719 it was bombarded by an English warship and had to be rebuilt.

You can see two Iron Age brochs at **Dun Telve** and **Dun Troddan**. Brochs are seen nowhere but in Scotland.

Oban is a major centre in the Western Highlands. It is a tourist town, fishing port and steamer and ferry terminal.

St Mary's Abbey is on Iona. St Columba lived here when he came from Ireland to convert the Scots to Christianity in AD 563.

Northern Scotland

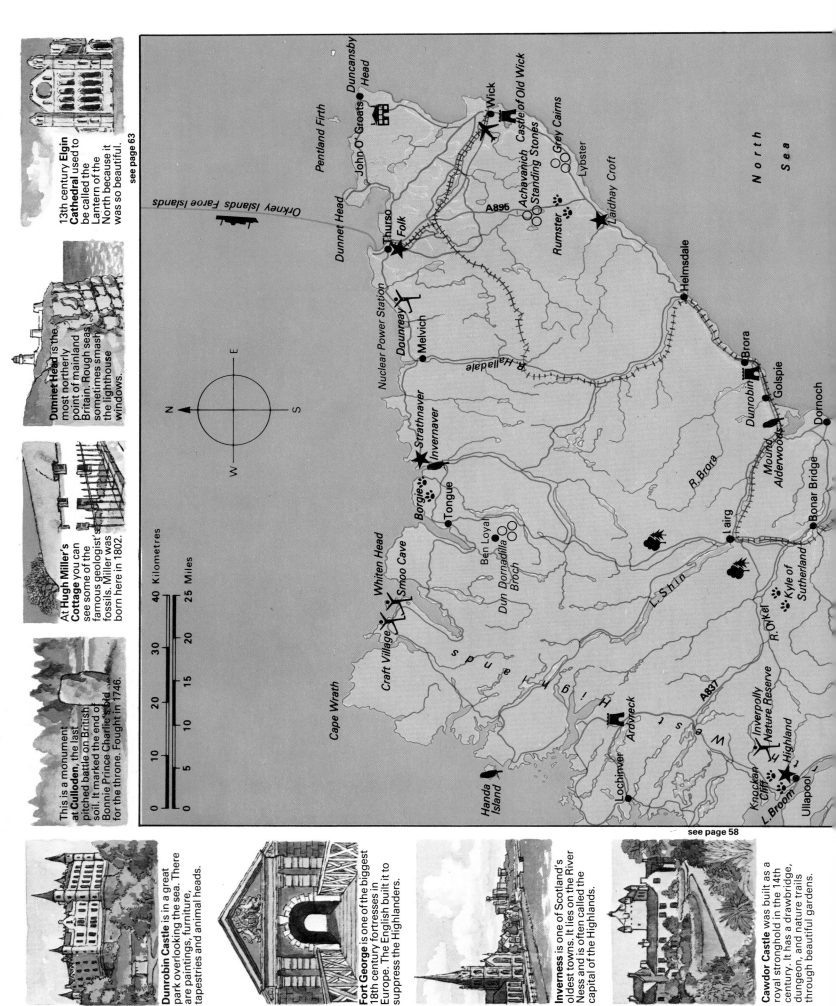

13th century **Elgin Cathedral** used to be called the Lantern of the North because it was so beautiful.

see page 63

Dunnet Head is the most northerly point of mainland Britain. Rough seas sometimes smash the lighthouse windows.

At **Hugh Miller's Cottage** you can see some of the famous geologist's fossils. Miller was born here in 1802.

This is a monument at **Culloden**, the last pitched battle on British soil. It marked the end of Bonnie Prince Charlie's bid for the throne. Fought in 1746.

Dunrobin Castle is in a great park overlooking the sea. There are paintings, furniture, tapestries and animal heads.

Fort George is one of the biggest 18th century fortresses in Europe. The English built it to suppress the Highlanders.

Inverness is one of Scotland's oldest towns. It lies on the River Ness and is often called the capital of the Highlands.

Cawdor Castle was built as a royal stronghold in the 14th century. It has a drawbridge, dungeon, and nature trails through beautiful gardens.

Map labels

Duncansby Head
John O'Groats
Wick
Castle of Old Wick
Standing Stones
Achavanich
Grey Cairns
Lybster
Pentland Firth
Laidhay Croft
Orkney Islands Faroe Islands
Dunnet Head
Thurso
Folk
A895
Rumster
North Sea
Nuclear Power Station
Dounreay
Melvich
Helmsdale
R. Halladale
Brora
Strathnaver
Invernaver
Golspie
Dunrobin
Borgie
Tongue
R. Brora
Mound
Alderwoods
Dornoch
Whiten Head
Smoo Cave
Ben Loyal
Dun Dornadilla Broch
Lairg
Bonar Bridge
Cape Wrath
Craft Village
S u t h e r l a n d
Kyle of Sutherland
L. Shin
R. Oykel
A837
Handa Island
Lochinver
Inverpolly Nature Reserve
Knockan Cliff
Highland
Ardvreck
A s s y n t
W e s t e r
L. Broom
Ullapool

N E S W

Kilometres
0 10 20 30 40
Miles
0 5 10 15 20 25

see page 58

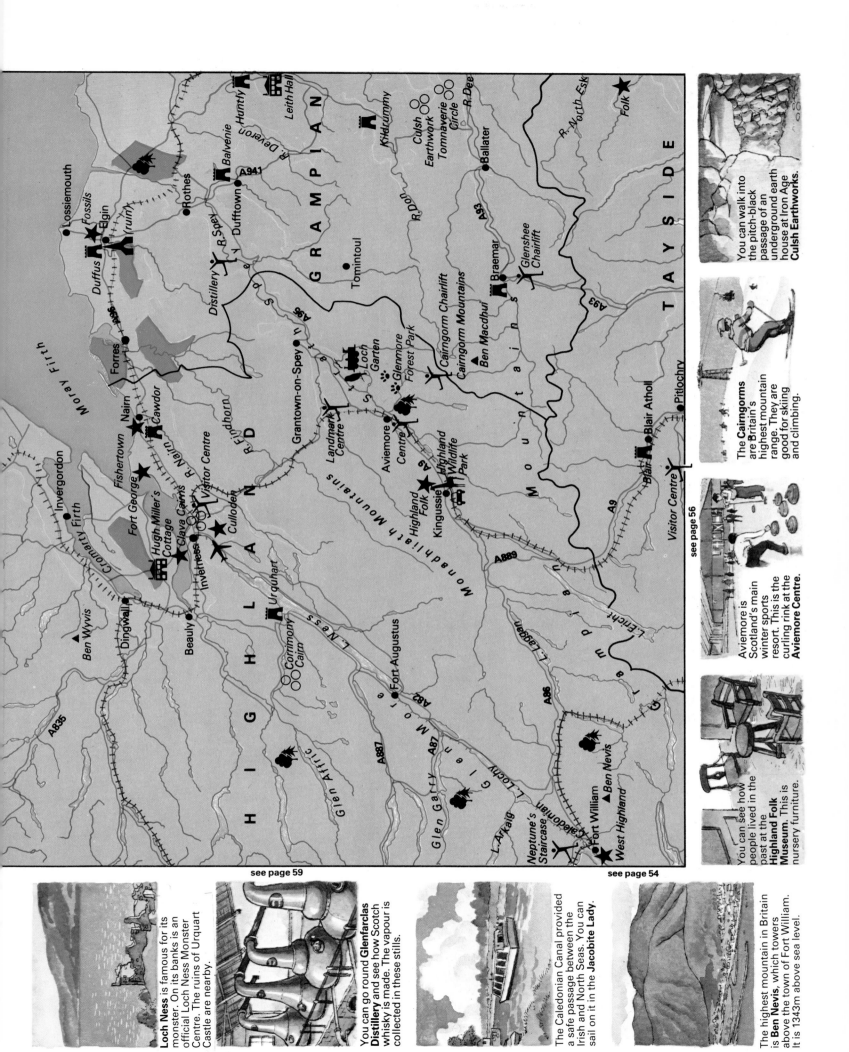

You can walk into the pitch-black passage of an underground earth house at Iron Age **Culsh Earthworks.**

The **Cairngorms** are Britain's highest mountain range. They are good for skiing and climbing.

Aviemore is Scotland's main winter sports resort. This is the curling rink at the **Aviemore Centre.**

You can see how people lived in the past at the **Highland Folk Museum.** This is nursery furniture.

Loch Ness is famous for its monster. On its banks is an official Loch Ness Monster Centre. The ruins of Urquart Castle are nearby.

You can go round **Glenfarclas Distillery** and see how Scotch whisky is made. The vapour is collected in these stills.

The Caledonian Canal provided a safe passage between the Irish and North Seas. You can sail on it in the **Jacobite Lady.**

The highest mountain in Britain is **Ben Nevis,** which towers above the town of Fort William. It is 1343m above sea level.

see page 59

see page 56

see page 54

61

Northern Ireland

The **Giant's Causeway** is a weird formation of volcanic rock which cooled into 6-sided columns.

Dunluce Castle was abandoned after the kitchen and cooks fell into the sea in a storm. There is a big cave below.

The **Ulster American Folk Park** tells the story of the many Irish settlers in the New World from the early 1700s on.

Lough Erne has over 150 wooded islands and is good for birdwatching. There are specially good heronries.

You can see the night sky projected on the dome of the **Planetarium** at Armagh. There is also a telescope you can work.

Navan Fort is Northern Ireland's most important ancient monument. It was the political capital of the prehistoric kings of Ulster.

You can go round **Belleek Pottery** and see how the porcelain is made. It first became famous in the 1800s.

Lough Neagh is the biggest lake in Britain (382 sq km). It is ideal for cruising, sailing, fishing and birdwatching.

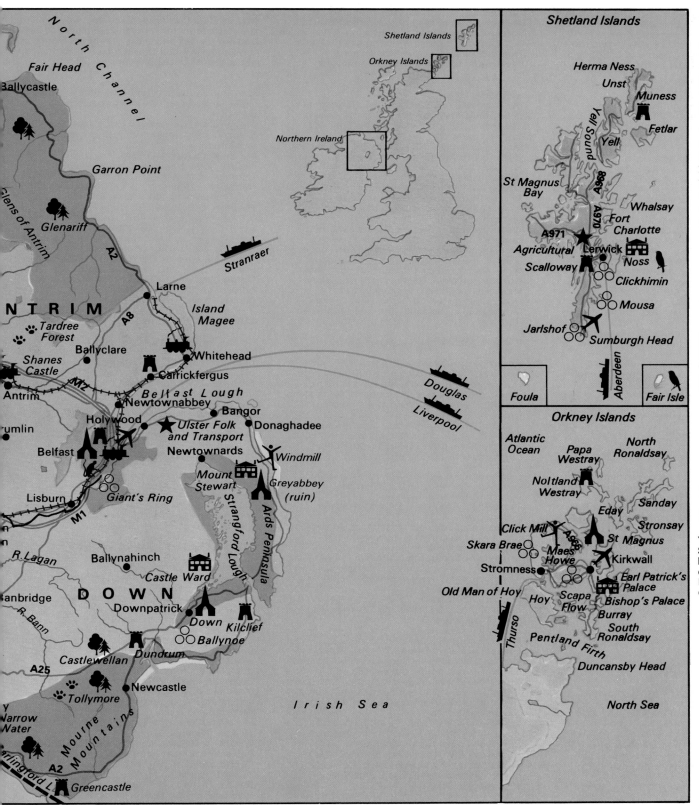

North Channel

Fair Head
Ballycastle

Garron Point

Glens of Antrim
Glenariff

A2

Stranraer

Larne

Island Magee

Tardree Forest
Ballyclare
Whitehead

Shanes Castle
Carrickfergus

Antrim

Belfast Lough
Newtownabbey
Holywood
Bangor
Donaghadee

Belfast
Ulster Folk and Transport
Newtownards

Lisburn
Giant's Ring
Mount Stewart
Windmill
Greyabbey (ruin)

Ballynahinch
Castle Ward

Banbridge
R. Lagan
R. Bann
Downpatrick
Down
Kilclief
Ballynoe

DOWN

A25
Castlewellan
Dundrum

Newcastle
Tollymore

Narrow Water
Mourne Mountains
A2
Greencastle

Irish Sea

Douglas
Liverpool

Shetland Islands
Orkney Islands
Northern Ireland

Shetland Islands

Herma Ness
Unst
Muness
Yell
Fetlar
St Magnus Bay
A968
Whalsay
Fort Charlotte
A970
A971
Agricultural
Lerwick
Scalloway
Noss
Clickhimin
Mousa
Jarlshof
Sumburgh Head

Foula
Aberdeen
Fair Isle

Orkney Islands

Atlantic Ocean
Papa Westray
North Ronaldsay
Noltland
Westray
Sanday
Eday
Stronsay
Click Mill
A966
Skara Brae
St Magnus
Maes Howe
Kirkwall
Stromness
Earl Patrick's Palace
Old Man of Hoy
Bishop's Palace
Hoy
Scapa Flow
Burray
South Ronaldsay
Thurso
Pentland Firth
Duncansby Head

North Sea

You can see remains of prehistoric, Dark Age and Viking villages at **Jarlshof**. These are Iron Age round houses.

Ferries to the Orkney Islands land at **Stromness**. There has been a harbour there since Viking times.

You can go on **Shanes Castle Railway** by the edge of Lough Neagh. There is a deer park too.

Carrickfergus Castle was begun in 1178 by the English. Life-size models now 'defend' it.

Belfast is the capital of Northern Ireland. The city hall was completed in 1906 and its copper dome is a landmark.

At the **Ulster Folk and Transport Museum** you can see a weaver's cottage, a spade mill, a forge, a school and a village church.

Ballycopeland Windmill is an 18th century corn grinding mill with wooden machinery. It is kept in working order.

This is the dining room of 18th century **Castle Ward**. There is also a Victorian laundry and a pastimes centre for children.

Gazetteer

On the following pages are some ideas for interesting places to visit throughout Britain. They are listed under their counties (which are in alphabetical order) and under the nearest town or village. You will be able to find the approximate position of many of the places mentioned on the maps in this book, but in order to find out exactly where they are you will need a good road atlas and sometimes an Ordnance Survey map too. Before setting out to visit any of the places, always try to get in touch with the tourist office which covers that area. They will be able to give you accurate information on opening hours, admission charges, and more detailed descriptions of the places and directions on how to get to them. You will find that many places are only open in the summer months, several are closed at least one day a week and some may only be open at weekends or in the afternoons. The addresses of the tourist boards are on page 79.

ENGLAND

AVON (Map page 45)

Bath. *American Museum.* See page 31.
Bath. *Henrietta Park.* Small park with a scented garden for the blind.
Bath. *Roman Baths.* See page 13.
Bath. *Roman Baths Museum.* Roman Baths complex and displays of relics.
Bath. *Museum of Costume.* See page 31.
Bath. *No 1, Royal Crescent.* Restored as an 18th century Georgian residence.
Bower Ashton. *Ashton Court Estate Nature Trail.* Junction A369 with B3124, entrance at Clifton Lodge Gate.
Bristol. *Bristol Industrial Museum.* Transport for land, sea and air, manufacturing equipment, working model railway.
Bristol. *Frome Valley Nature Trail.*
Bristol. *SS Great Britain.* First propeller-driven, ocean-going, iron ship. Designed in 1843 by Brunel. You can go on board.
Rode, nr Bath. *The Tropical Bird Gardens.* In grounds of Rode Manor. About 1,000 birds of 240 species.
Trowbridge. *Farleigh Castle.* Ruined 14th century castle with chapel and monuments.
Weston-Super-Mare. *Steep Holm Island.* Nature reserve, 8km offshore.

BEDFORDSHIRE (Map page 48)

Biggleswade. *The Shuttleworth Collection.* See page 31.
Dunstable. *Whipsnade Wild Animal Park.* See page 30.
Leighton Buzzard. *Leighton Buzzard Narrow Gauge Railway.* Steam, diesel and petrol locomotives from all over the world.
Luton. *Luton Hoo.* Exterior by Robert Adam, 1767, interior remodelled early in 20th century. Contains pictures, furniture, tapestries, china, Russian jewels and mementoes of Russian Imperial Family. Gardens.
Stagsden. *Stagsden Bird Gardens.*
Woburn. *Woburn Abbey.* Contains paintings, porcelain, furniture and silver. In the grounds are a pottery, antiques centre, maze and Chinese dairy.
Woburn. *Woburn Abbey Deer Park.* See page 49.
Woburn. *Woburn Wild Animal Kingdom.* Many endangered species and exotic animals. Pets' corner.

BERKSHIRE (Map page 40)

Maidenhead. *Courage Shire Horse Centre.* See page 40.
Pangbourne. *Basildon Park.* Classical 1776 house with unusual Octagon Room and Shell Room. Over 400 acres of park and woodland.
Reading. *Museum of English Rural Life.* 150 years of history of the English countryside including farm and village life, crafts and household utensils.
Wargrave. *Dean Place Farm Trail, Crazies Hill.* Warren Row turning off A423, between Henley and Maidenhead.
Windsor. *Royal Windsor Safari Park.* See page 40.
Windsor. *Windsor Castle.* See page 14.

BUCKINGHAMSHIRE (Map pages 40 and 48)

Beaconsfield. *Bekonscot Model Village.* See page 30.
High Wycombe. *Wycombe Chair and Local History Museum.* Includes chairs of most periods, also Buckinghamshire lace.
Middle Claydon, nr Winslow. *Claydon House.* Includes *Florence Nightingale Museum.*
Newport Pagnell. *Chicheley Hall.* Built 1720s. Contains Classical hall, panelled rooms, hidden library, *Beatty Naval Museum.* Gardens with formal lake.
Old Bradwell, nr Milton Keynes. *Nature trail from Bradwell Windmill to Bradwell Abbey.* See *Bancroft Roman Villa* and the concrete cows on the way.
Olney. *Flamingo Gardens and Zoological Park.*
Quainton, nr Aylesbury. *Buckinghamshire Railway Centre.* Britain's largest private railway collection. Steam train rides.
Stacey Hill Farm, nr Wolverton. *The Milton Keynes Museum of Industry and Rural Life.* Exhibition of industrial, agricultural and domestic items.
West Wycombe. *West Wycombe Park.* 18th century house with many painted ceilings. Gardens contain temples and a swan-shaped lake.
Wing. *Ascott House.* Contains furniture and Oriental porcelain. Gardens include topiary, sundial, water-lilies and unusual trees.
Great Linford. *Linford Wood Trail.* Turn off Monks Way to the south and take signposted trackway.

CAMBRIDGESHIRE (Map pages 48-49)

Arrington, nr Royston. *Wimpole Hall, Farm and Park.* Mansion dates from 300 years ago. Home farm with rare breeds. Woodland play area.
Bourn, nr Cambridge. *Bourn Post-Mill.* Possibly the oldest post-mill in England. You can go inside.
Cambridge. *Cambridge and County Folk Museum.* Agricultural and domestic exhibits, including toys from 1650 to present-day.
Cambridge. *Cambridge Brass Rubbing Centre, Castle Street.*
Cambridge. *Fitzwilliam Museum.* Contains paintings, furniture, clocks, Egyptian collection, coins and medals.
Cambridge. *Coe Fen and Paradise Island Nature Trails.*
Cambridge. *Sedgwick Museum of Geology.* Contains fossils from all over the world and different kinds of rocks.
Duxford, nr Cambridge. *Imperial War Museum.* In hangars dating from World War I. Has over 100 historic and modern aircraft, including a model of Concorde.
Ely. *Stretham Engine.* Giant, steam-powered, beam engine. Erected in 1831 to drain Fens.
Ely. *Ely Cathedral.*
Linton. *Linton Zoo.*
Lode. *Anglesey Abbey and Gardens.*
Peakirk, nr Peterborough. *Peakirk Waterfowl Gardens.* Includes flamingos and 105 different kinds of ducks, geese and swans.
Stamford (Lincs.). *Burghley House.* One of the largest and grandest Elizabethan houses. Built 1565-1578. About 240 rooms, including the Heaven Room.
Wansford. *Nene Valley Steam Railway.* Collection includes European locomotives. Signal box open for inspection.
Wicken, nr Ely. *Wicken Fen Nature Trails.* Walks through Nature Reserve. Look out for fen cottage and drainage pump. Signposted from Wicken village on A1123.

CHESHIRE (Map page 47)

Chester. *Grosvenor Museum.* Roman remains including Roman army display. Also art, folk-life and natural history exhibitions.
Chester. *Roman Amphitheatre.* Has an excavated underground chamber which is laid out as a garden with Roman pillars.
Congleton. *Little Moreton Hall.* See page 47.
Disley. *Lyme Park.* Elizabethan house, with later additions. Country Park with adventure playground, nature trails and deer.
Ellesmere Port. *Ellesmere Port Boat Museum.* Traditional canal boats, boatbuilding and repair tools. Also 1830s cottages and pumphouse, blacksmith and canal trips.
Knutsford. *Tatton Park.* Georgian mansion showing life upstairs and downstairs. Working 1930s farm. Adventure playground and deer park.
Macclesfield. *Gawsworth Hall.* Tudor, box-framed manor house with pictures, sculpture, and furniture.
Macclesfield. *Jodrell Bank.* See page 47.
Malpas. *Cholmondeley Castle Gardens.* Gardens, farm with rare breeds of animals.
Nantwich. *Bridgemere Wildlife Park.* Birds of prey, waterfowl and British animals.
Poynton, nr Bramhall. *Poynton Farm Trails, Towers Road.* East of A523, south of Bramhall.
Styal. *Quarry Bank Mill.* 18th century cotton mill and cottages. Includes the apprentice house as in 1830s. Exhibition of cotton industry.
Tarporley. *Beeston Castle.* 13th century castle with dry moat. Also castle museum.
Upton-by-Chester. *Chester Zoo.* Animals in outdoor enclosures, free-flight aviary, tropical house, aquarium and waterbus trips.

CLEVELAND (Map page 50)

Coulby Newham, Middlesbrough. *Newham Grange Leisure Farm.* Working farm with rare breeds of animals, farm trail, nature trail and old shops.
Hartlepool. *Maritime Museum.* Maritime history of Hartlepool, including shipbuilding, fishing and marine engineering.
Stewart Park, Middlesbrough. *Captain Cook Birthplace Museum.* Displays of natural history and artefacts tell the story of Cook's early life and voyages.
Redcar. *The Zetland Lifeboat Museum.* Zetland is the oldest surviving lifeboat in the world. Displays relate to sea rescue and the local fishing industry. Marine aquarium.
Stockton-on-Tees. *Preston Hall Museum.* Social history museum including old street and rooms, toy gallery, armoury and transport exhibits. Also park with zoo and riverside walk.

CORNWALL (Map page 42)

Calstock. *Cotehele House.* Tudor house with armour, banners and original furniture. Garden has water-mill, and blacksmith and wheelwright shops. The *Maritime Museum* on the quay includes a restored barge.
Camborne. *Camborne School of Mines Museum.* Worldwide mineral and ore collections.
Camborne. *Cornish Engines, East Pool Mine.* A beam, winding engine and a beam, pumping engine.
Dobwalls. *Family Adventure Park.* Most extensive miniature railway in Europe. Adventure playgrounds and *Countryside Museum and Gallery.*
Gulval, nr Penzance. *Chysauster Ancient British Village.* See page 12.
Gweek, nr Helston. *Cornish Seal Sanctuary.* Ten pools with at least 30 seals. Conservation Centre, pollution display and aquarium. Also a Seal Hospital.
Helston. *Flambards Theme Park.* Includes a Victorian village, 'Britain in the Blitz' and an aeropark displaying aircraft and aviation history. Adventure playgrounds and rides.
Helston. *Goonhilly Satellite Earth Station.* Two big aerials which receive signals from space satellites. Visitors' centre, adventure playground and Lizard Nature Reserve.
Helston. *Helston Museum.* Folk Museum.
Looe. *Murrayton Monkey Sanctuary.*
Lostwithiel. *Restormel Castle.* Built in 1100, last occupied during the Civil War. Ruins include the Great Hall, curtain wall and well.
Newlyn East, nr Camborne. *Lappa Valley Railway.*
Polperro. *Model Village.*
St Agnes. *Leisure Park.* Cornwall, dinosaurs and fairyland in miniature.

CUMBRIA (Map pages 52-53)

Ambleside. *Rydal Mount.* Poet Wordsworth's home from 1813-1850.
Appleby-in-Westmorland. *Appleby Castle Conservation Centre.* Rare farm animals and large collection of birds in the grounds. Norman Keep and Great Hall.
Bassenthwaite. *Dodd Wood Nature Trail.*
Bowness-On-Windermere. *Windermere Steamboat Museum.* Victorian and Edwardian steam, sailing, and motor boats. Includes *The Amazon* dinghy and Captain Flint's houseboat from *Swallows and Amazons* and Beatrix Potter's rowing boat.
Brantwood. *Brantwood Nature Trail.* East side of Coniston Water.
Brockhole, Windermere. *Brockhole - Lake District National Park Centre.* Displays on the Lake District from prehistoric times to the present. Activity trails, adventure playground, landscaped grounds, circular lake cruises, family events.
Cark-in-Cartmel, nr Grange-Over-Sands. *Holker Hall.* 16th century house with 19th century additions. Gardens include an adventure playground and Amazing Coloured Maze. Also of interest is the *Lakeland Motor Museum.*
Carlisle. *Eden Riverside Trail.* Start at Eden Bridge, Bitts Park in Carlisle.
Castlerigg. *Castlerigg Stone Circle.* Almost complete Bronze Age circle, 30m across.
Eskdale. *Hardknott Castle.* Remains of a Roman fort.
Finsthwaite. *Stott Park Bobbin Mill.* Restored, working mill.
Grasmere. *The Wordsworth Museum, Dove Cottage.* Home of poet Wordsworth from 1799 to 1808.
Hawkshead. *Grizedale Forest Park and Centre.* Exhibition of 2,000 years of forestry. Land arts collection and craft gallery. Trails and cycle hire. 'Animal' playground.
Kendal. *Levens Hall.* See page 53.
Kendal. *Serpentine Woods Nature Trail.* Starting point in Serpentine Road.
Kendal. *Abbot Hall Art Gallery and Museum.* Georgian house furnished as in 1760 with many fine paintings of the lakes and fells. Also *The Museum of Lakeland Life and Industry.* Displays Lakeland history in farmhouse rooms and reconstructed workshops. Rooms devoted to Arthur Ransome (author of *Swallows and Amazons*) and John Cunliffe (author of *Postman Pat* and *Rosie & Jim*).
Kendal. *Kendal Museum of Natural History and Archaeology.* One of the earliest museums in Britain, dating from 1796.
Keswick. *Friars Crag Nature Trail.* Starting point is at the municipal car park.
Lakeside - Haverthwaite, nr Newby Bridge. *Lakeside and Haverthwaite Railway.* Standard gauge railway. The station at Lakeside connects with the Windermere steamers.
Penrith. *Dalemain.* Medieval, Elizabethan and Georgian house. Countryside and agriculture museum, deer park and secret 'Mrs Mouse's House'.
Penrith. *Hutton-in-the-Forest.* Built in the 14th century, with later additions. Contents include furniture, armour, tapestries, paintings, plasterwork ceilings and carvings. Grounds include lakes, woods, a dovecote and a walled garden.
Penrith. *Lowther Leisure Park.* Miniature railway, adventure playgrounds, sporting activities. Rides include a giant slide. Red deer park.
Ravenglass. *Muncaster Castle.* 13th century castle, full of treasures. 77 acres of gardens include a nature trail and wild flower meadow. Also an owl centre, wildfowl pond and adventure playground.
Ravenglass-Dalegarth. *Ravenglass and Eskdale Railway.* Narrow gauge railway. Also the *Ravenglass Railway Museum.*

DERBYSHIRE (Map pages 47, 48 and 51)

Bakewell. *Chatsworth.* Built 1555, with later additions. You can see the state rooms, a sculpture gallery, library, pictures, furniture and domestic relics. The 100-acre park, landscaped by Capability Brown, includes lakes, fountains, a tropical greenhouse and a rose garden.
Bakewell. *Chatsworth Farmyard and Adventure Playground.* See page 51.
Bakewell. *Haddon Hall.* Medieval manor house. Tudor panelled dining room, painted ceilings, 14th century chapel with wall paintings. Also the giants' kitchens from the BBC *Narnia* series. Terraced rose gardens.
Bakewell. *The Old House Museum.* Includes 19th century costumes, Victorian kitchen, toys, cameras, tools and local historical items.
Bradwell, nr Hathersage. *Bagshawe Caverns.* Water-worn passage with fossils, stalagmites and stalactites. Torchlight explorations.
Castleton, nr Hathersage. *Peak Cavern.* Huge floodlit natural cavern.
Crich, nr Matlock. *The Tramway Museum.* See page 31.
Dale Abbey, Ilkeston. *The Cat and Fiddle Mill.* 4-sail, wooden post-mill built in 1788. In working order.
Derby. *Derby City Museum and Art Gallery.* Exhibitions include costumes, coins and medals, toys and model theatres.
Derby. *Derby Industrial Museum.* Rolls-Royce collection of historic aero-engines plus the industrial history of Derbyshire. Working scale model of the Midland Railway.
Derby. *Pickford's House.* Museum of Georgian life.
Doe Lea, nr Chesterfield. *Hardwick Hall.* Elizabethan house with 16th century furniture and tapestries. Needlework, some sewn by Mary Queen of Scots while a prisoner at the Hall. Park includes a nature walk.
Elvaston, nr Derby. *Elvaston Castle Country Park.* Parklands with lakeside nature trail, and *Elvaston Castle Countryside Museum.*
Kedleston, Derby. *Kedleston Hall.* Robert Adam house begun in 1759. Contains a marble hall, furnished state rooms and an *Indian Museum* with silver and ivory collections.
Matlock. *Heights of Abraham.* Country park reached by cable car. Tours of the *Rutland* and *Great Masson* caves. Display on the story of lead mining. Children's play area.
Matlock. *Riber Castle Wildlife Park, Riber Castle.* Rare and endangered species of birds and animals, including lynx.
Matlock Bath. *Gulliver's Kingdom.* Family attractions and rides.
Sudbury, Derby. *Sudbury Hall Museum of Childhood.*
Via Gellia, nr Cromford. *Good Luck Lead Mine.* An underground lead-mining museum.

DEVON (Map pages 42-43)

Appledore. *North Devon Maritime Museum.*
Babbacome, Torquay. *Model Village.*
Barnstaple. *Arlington Court.* Illustrates the life and hobbies of an unusual Victorian lady. Collections include shells, model ships and horse-drawn vehicles. Gardens and lake.
Bickleigh, nr Tiverton. *Bickleigh Castle.* Inhabited, moated stronghold, important in the Civil War. Cromwellian armoury, 11th century chapel, 17th century farm house, Tudor bedroom, 'spooky tower'. *Domestic Museum* with period rocking horses to ride. *Mary Rose* and *Titanic* exhibitions. World War II spy and escape gadgets.
Bickleigh, nr Tiverton. *The Devonshire Centre.* A restored working water-mill and a farm worked by traditional methods.
Buckfastleigh - Totnes-Riverside. *South Devon Railway.* Steam train rides.
Budleigh Salterton. *Bicton Park.* 18th century garden with tropical/cacti house, countryside museum and woodland railway.
Cowley Wood, Parracombe. *Cowley Cleave Nature Trail.* Off A399 between Ilfracombe and Blackmore Gate. Start at Cowley Wood car park.
Dartmouth. *Newcomen Engine House.* One of the first steam-engines, built by Newcomen, and still in working order.
Drewsteignton, nr Chagford. *Castle Drogo.* Built early this century. Terraced garden and walks.
Dunsford, nr Exeter. *Dunsford Nature Trail.* Start at Steps Bridge, near Dunsford on the B3212, west of Exeter.
Exeter. *Killerton House and Gardens.* 18th century house with a collection of costumes. Hillside gardens.
Morwellham, nr Tavistock. *Morwellham Quay.* Port restored to 1860s. Victorian farmyard. Tramway ride into copper mine. Workshops and workers' cottages. Hydro-electric power station. Port and mining museums.
Paignton. *Paignton Zoo and Botanical Gardens.*
Paignton. *Dartmouth Steam Railway.* Great Western Railway steam train rides.
Plymouth. *Buckland Abbey.* Sir Francis Drake galleries and display showing story of the abbey. Medieval barn where you can see craftspeople at work.
Plymouth. *Plymouth Aquarium.*
Plympton, nr Plymouth. *Saltram House.* George II house incorporating an old Tudor mansion.
Powderham. *Powderham Castle.* Built 1390. Rose garden, deer park.
Salcombe. *Overbeck's.* A museum including ships and shipbuilding displays, plus 19th century photographs, dolls and dolls' furniture. A secret room and gardens.
Sparkwell, nr Plymouth. *Dartmoor Wildlife Park.*
Tiverton. *Tiverton Castle.* Norman fortress with Civil War armour to try on. Medieval gatehouse and tower, New World tapestry, clock collection and secret passages.
Torcross, nr Kingsbridge. *Slapton Sands Nature Trail.* Turn off A379 at north end of Slapton Sands, and start at Strete Gate.
Torquay. *Kents Cavern.* One of Europe's most important sites for prehistoric remains.
Totnes. *Devonshire Collection of Period Costume.*

DORSET (Map pages 40 and 43)

Beaminster. *Parnham House.* Tudor manor house with furniture-making workshops and exhibitions by designers, artists and local craftspeople.
Bournemouth-Poole. *Compton Acres.* 7 different gardens, including Japanese, Italian, rock, water and a Heather Dell.
Bovington Camp, nr Wool. *The Tank Museum.* Over 200 tanks and armoured cars.
Brownsea Island. *Brownsea Island Nature Reserve.* Take a boat from Poole Quay or Sandbanks. Includes herons, terns, red squirrels and peacocks. Nature trail.
Cerne Abbas. *Cerne Giant.* Huge figure cut into the chalk hillside.
Corfe. *Corfe Castle.* Ruins of a castle begun in the 11th century.
Dorchester. *Maiden Castle.* See page 12.
Milton Abbas. *Park Farm Museum.* Historic brewing implements, farming relics and chimney-pot display. Farmyard animals.
Puddletown, nr Dorchester. *Athelhampton.* 15th century house with great hall, state bedroom, 8 walled gardens and a dovecote.
Sherborne. *Sherborne New Castle.* 16th century mansion house, including dungeon and suits of armour. Grounds by Capability Brown.
Sherborne. *Worldwide Butterflies, Compton House.* See page 31.
Wimborne Minster. *Wimborne Model Town.*

CO. DURHAM (Map pages 50 and 52-53)

Barnard Castle. *The Bowes Museum.* Includes more than 30 galleries of art and antiques from every country in Europe. Rooms of costume, toys and musical instruments.
Beamish, nr Chester-le-Street. *North of England Open Air Museum.* See page 31.
Darlington. *Darlington Railway Centre and Museum.* See page 50.
Derwent Country Park. *Derwent Walk.* From Blackhill to Swalwell roundabout.
Durham. *Durham Castle.* Built from about 1070.
Durham. *Durham Cathedral.* See page 50.
Shilton. *Timothy Hackworth's Victorian Railway Museum.* Restored home, workshop and engine shed illustrate the life and work of this steam locomotive pioneer. Railtrail walkways.
Staindrop, Darlington. Raby Castle. See page 52.

EAST SUSSEX (Map page 41)

Alfriston. *Drusilla's.* Zoo park, pottery, miniature railway, adventure playground and farmyard.
Battle. *Battle Abbey.* See page 41.
Battle. *Battle Museum.* Diorama of the Battle of Hastings and a reproduction of part of the Bayeux Tapestry. There are also Roman remains.
Brighton. *Brighton Sea Life Centre.* British and tropical marine species. Europe's largest underwater tunnel.
Brighton. *Pirates Deep.* Indoor nautical adventure play centre - up to 12 years.
Brighton. *Royal Pavilion.* See page 18.
Brighton. *St Bartholomew's Church.* England's tallest parish church.
Burwash. *Bateman's.* Home of author Rudyard Kipling from 1902-1936. His study is kept as it was. Restored working water-mill and gardens.
Eastbourne. *Royal National Lifeboat Institute Museum.* Includes models of lifeboats, old rescue equipment etc.
Eastbourne. *Tower 73.* Display about Martello towers housed in a restored Martello tower.
Exceat, nr Seaford. *Seven Sisters Country Park Trail.* On A259 Eastbourne to Seaford road at Exceat Bridge over River Cuckmere. Yearly running marathon.
Hailsham. *Michelham Priory.* 13th century priory surrounded by moat. Contains furniture, tapestries, musical instruments and stained glass. Also has forge, wheelwright's museum and a restored working medieval water-mill.
Halland, nr Lewes. *Bentley Wildfowl Park.* Over 100 species of bird. Also a Tudor farmhouse with farm animals. Adventure playground, miniature railway, woodland walk.
Sheffield Park-New Coombe Bridge, nr Uckfield. *Bluebell Railway.* Vintage steam trains, museum and locomotive shed.
Hove. *Brighton and Hove Engineerium.* Steam museum with full-size and model engines.
Lewes. *Anne of Cleves' House.* Museum of local history with household equipment, furniture, Sussex ironwork and pottery.
Lewes. *Castle.* Keep of Norman stronghold with 14th century Barbican. Museum of archaeological finds from East Sussex. Model of Lewes town as it was in 1800.
Rye. *Model Son et Lumière.* A scale model of Rye with special lighting, music and voices telling the history of the town. Local history exhibition.
Rye. *Rye Museum.* Housed in *Wpres Castle*. Dungeons, gun garden with replica cannon and sentry walkway. 18th century fire-engine. Includes toys and dolls.
Sedlescombe. *Norton's Farm Museum.* 5km north of Hastings on A21.

ESSEX (Map pages 41 and 49)

Colchester. *Colchester Castle Museum.* See page 49.
Colchester. *Colchester Zoo.* Over 150 species. Also pets' corner and miniature railway.
Colchester. *Hollytrees Museum.* Two centuries of toys, costume, decorative arts and curios in a Georgian town house.
Colchester. *Natural History Museum.* Exhibitions and displays on the local wildlife and geography in the former *All Saints Church*.
Grays Thurrock. *Thurrock Museum.* History of local River Thames and surrounding area from prehistoric to recent times.
Halstead. *Gosfield Hall.* Elizabethan house with Tudor well and pumphouse. 1540 long gallery.
Harlow. *Greenway's Netteswell Trail.* Starts from Study and Visitor Centre, Second Avenue.
Harwich. *Harwich Redoubt.* Circular fort built in 1808 as coastal defence against Napoleon. Includes a moat, cells, cannons and museum of local finds.
Saffron Walden. *Audley End House.* See page 49.
Upminster, nr Romford. *Upminster Mill.* Smock mill built in 1803 still with its original machinery. Guided tours.
Widdington. *Mole Hall Wildlife Park.* Includes a butterfly pavillion.

GLOUCESTERSHIRE (Map page 45)

Berkeley. *Berkeley Castle.* Norman fortress with terraced Elizabethan gardens, Elizabeth I's

bowling green and cell where Edward II was murdered. Butterfly farm.
Bourton-on-the-Water. *Birdland.*
Bourton-on-the-Water. *Cotswold Motor Museum.* Includes toy collection, rebuilt shops and garages.
Bourton-on-the-Water. *Model Railway Exhibition.*
Bourton-on-the-Water. *Model Village.*
Charlton Abbots. *Belas Knap Long Barrow.* 55m long barrow with three burial chambers.
Chedworth. *Denfurlong Farm Trail.* Shows landforms, crops and animals. Turn off A429 to Chedworth. Route is also signposted from Withington, off A435 or A436.
Cheltenham. *Cotswold Farm Park.* Rare breeds of British farm animals, farm trail, pets' corner and adventure playground.
Chipping Campden. *Woolstaplers Hall Museum.* Includes a 1920s dolls' house, cobbler's shop, early photographic/cinematographic collections, dentists' instruments.
Cirencester. *Corinium Museum.* Fine collection of Roman antiquities. Reconstructions recreate the way of life in Roman Britain's second largest town.
Coleford. *Clearwell Caves Ancient Iron Mines.* Iron was first mined here nearly 3,000 years ago. 8 large caverns with displays of mineral samples and mining equipment. Also several vintage engines in working order.
Gloucester. *Beatrix Potter Museum.* Life of Beatrix Potter shown by displays of belongings and works.
Gloucester. *Bishop Hooper's Lodging.* 3 medieval, timber-framed buildings displaying local history, crafts and industries. Dairy, workshops, Victorian classroom and herb garden.
Gloucester. *Gloucester Cathedral.*
Gloucester. *Prinknash Bird Park.*
Lydney. *Norchard Steam Centre.* Includes steam locomotives, steam cranes, and a railway museum. You can go for rides on 'steam days'.
Newent. *The National Birds of Prey Centre.* See page 31.
Slimbridge. *The Wildfowl and Wetlands Trust.* See page 31.
Snowshill, nr Broadway. *Snowshill Manor.* Tudor house. A collection of craftsmanship includes toys, clocks, musical instruments, bicycles and armour.
Winchcombe. *Sudeley Castle.* See page 45.
Yanworth. *Chedworth Roman Villa.* Remains of Roman villa with baths and mosaic floors and museum displaying relics found at the site.

GREATER MANCHESTER (Map page 47)

Bolton. *Smithills Hall Nature Trail.* Start at *Smithills Hall Museum* in Bolton.
Manchester. *Museum of Science and Industry.* 14 galleries with hundreds of working exhibits. Space gallery and hands-on science centre.
Prestwich, Manchester. *Heaton Hall.* House built in 1772, contains period paintings and furniture.
Rusholm, Manchester. *The Gallery of English Costume, Platt Hall.* Clothes and accessories from 15th century to the present-day.
Salford. *Museum and Art Gallery.* Includes a reconstructed, 19th century street and paintings by L.S. Lowry.
Wigan. *Wigan Pier.* Heritage centre, living museum, world's largest working steam-engine, canal trips.

HAMPSHIRE (Map page 40)

Alresford. *The Mid-Hants 'Watercress' Line.* Steam locomotives. Steam rides.
Andover. *The Hawk Conservancy.* Birds of prey including falcons, eagles, owls. Flying demonstrations. Woodland garden.
Beaulieu. *Maritime Museum, Buckler's Hard.* See page 31.
Beaulieu. *National Motor Museum.* See page 31.
Burlesdon. *Manor Farm and Upper Hamble County Park.* Agricultural history of Hampshire from 1850-1950. Traditional farm buildings and animals, including shire horses. Shoreline walks, woods and meadows.
Butser, nr Petersfield. *Butser Ancient Farm.* See page 12.

Fordingbridge. *Breamore House.* Elizabethan manor house. Also *Carriage Museum* and *Countryside Museum* with farm cottage and workshops.
Liphook. *Hollycombe Steam Collection.* Steam railways, steam swings, tramway and steam fairground. Woodland gardens and arboretum.
Litchfield. *Beacon Hill.* Hill fort.
Portchester. *Portchester Castle.* See page 40.
Portsmouth. *H.M.S. Victory.* See page 30. Also the *Mary Rose.*
Portsmouth. *The Portsmouth Royal Naval Museum.* History of the Royal Navy from its earliest days to the Falklands campaign.
nr Reading. *Wellington Country Park.* Deer park, Thames Valley time trail, miniature steam railway, children's farmyard, adventure playground, nature trails. Also the *National Dairy Museum.*
Selborne. *The Wakes.* Collections relating to the naturalist Gilbert White and to the explorers Frank and Lawrence Oates. Lawrence Oates was a member of Scott's failed South Pole expedition.
Stratfield Saye, nr Reading. *Stratfield Saye House.* Exhibition on the first Duke of Wellington. Wildfowl sanctuary.
Winchester. *Marwell Zoological Park.* Nearly 1000 animals and birds. Adventure playground, miniature railway and children's farmyard.

HEREFORD/WORCESTER (Map page 45)

Alfrick, nr Worcester. *Ravenshill Woodland Reserve Trail.* Take the A44 west from Worcester, turn left after crossing River Terne at Knightsford Bridge and follow Alfrick signposts.
Bewdley. *Bewdley Museum.* Displays of various crafts including potter's and weaver's craftshops and brass foundry.
Bewdley. *Severn Valley Railway.* Over 30 steam locomotives. Riverside walks and picnic areas.
Bewdley. *West Midlands Safari and Leisure Park.*
Bromsgrove. *Avoncroft Museum of Buildings.* Old buildings, including a working windmill and box-framed houses.
Eardisland, nr Leominster. *Burton Court.* Costume exhibition and model fairground.
Hartlebury, nr Kidderminster. *Hartlebury Castle.* State rooms open to the public. Also *Hereford and Worcester County Museum.*
Hereford. *Bulmer Railway Centre.* Displays of steam locomotives with occasional 'steam days'.
Honeybourne, nr Evesham. *The Domestic Fowl Trust.* Over 150 rare breeds of ducks, geese, hens, turkeys etc.
Kingsland, Leominster. *Croft Castle.* Dates back to the late 13th century. Nearby is the Iron Age fort of *Croft Ambrey.*
Malvern Wells. *Hereford Beacon.* Large hill fort.

HERTFORDSHIRE (Map pages 40-41 and 48-49)

Hatfield. *Hatfield House.* See page 18.
Hatfield. *Mill Green Museum and Water-mill.* 18th century restored working water-mill. Local history and craft exhibitions in the miller's house.
Hertford. *Hertford Museum.* Exhibits of local geology, archaeology and natural history in a 17th century building. Also an early 17th century knot garden.
Knebworth. *Knebworth House.* See page 18.
Letchworth. *Standalone Farm.* Open working farm. Domestic animals, milking demonstrations, resident blacksmith.
St Albans. *St Albans Abbey.* Begun in 11th century, it has second longest nave in England and rare medieval wall paintings discovered behind old whitewash.
St Albans. *St Albans Roman (Verulamium) Museum.* See page 12.
St Albans. *Verulamium Roman Theatre.* Britain's only completely exposed Roman theatre.
St Albans. *Verulamium Roman Town.* See page 13.
Tring. *Tring Reservoirs Nature Trail.* Turn off A41, between Tring and Aylesbury, on to B489. Nature Reserve car park is beyond Buckland at Startops End. Very good for birdwatching.
Tring. *Zoological Museum.*
Watford. *Cassiobury Park.* Nature trail along

Grand Union Canal, with ornamental stone bridge. Narrow boat trips and miniature railway.
Welwyn. The Roman Bath House. Preserved in a specially constructed vault under the A1(M).

HUMBERSIDE (Map pages 50-51)

Beverley. *Skidby Mill.* Well-preserved working windmill, built in 1821. Also museum and craft workshop.
Bridlington. *Burton Agnes Hall.* Elizabethan country house. Walled garden with giant board games. Also pets' corner.
Bridlington. *Sewerby Hall and Park.* Museum and art gallery. Zoo and gardens, children's park and putting.
Brigg. *Elsham Hall, Country Park.* Falconry centre, children's farm, carp-feeding jetty and pets' corner. Working craft centre and wild butterfly garden walkway.
Burton Constable, nr Hull. *Burton Constable.* See page 51.
Driffield. *Sledmere House.* 1787 Georgian house including furniture and paintings. Capability Brown gardens and park.
Hull. *Town Docks Museum.* Displays about fishing, whaling and shipping.
Hull. *The Streetlife Museum.* Transport displays and street scenes. Old vehicles.
Hull. *The Hull & East Riding Museum.* Archaeological displays including Roman and Celtic.
Hull. *Wilberforce House and Georgian Houses.* Has collections relating to slavery and furniture, costumes and silver.
Scunthorpe. *Normanby Hall.* Completed 1830, Regency style. Victorian school room, costume gallery, transport display and farming museum. Country park with miniature railway, aviary and deer.

ISLE OF MAN (Map page 53)

Ballaugh. *Curraghs Wild Life Park.* Animals from around the world. Nature trail to *Curraghs Wetlands.*
Castletown. *Castle Rushen.* Medieval fortress.
Castletown. *Nautical Museum.* Housed in an old boathouse, includes *Peggy,* a schooner-rigged, armed yacht built in 1791.
Cregneash. *Cregneash Open Air Folk Museum.* Buildings show life of a crofting, fishing community at the turn of the century. Includes a traditional working farm and craft demonstrations.
Douglas. *Douglas Horse Tramway.* Horse-drawn tramway from Victoria Pier to Manx Electric Railway Station.
Douglas. *The Manx Museum.* National Art Gallery, archaeology and natural history displays, social history galleries.
Douglas-Laxey. *Manx Electric Railway.* Narrow gauge railway.
Douglas-Port Erin. *Isle of Man Railway.* Narrow gauge steam railway.
Laxey. *The Lady Isabella Wheel.* See page 53.
Laxey. *Snaefell Mountain Railway.* Narrow gauge railway to top of Snaefell, the island's highest mountain.
Ramsey. *'The Grove' Rural Life Museum.* An early Victorian house and outbuildings, with horse-driven threshing mill, old vehicles and agricultural equipment plus some livestock.
Snaefell Mountain. *Murrays Motorcycle Museum.* Over 130 motorcycles from 1902 and 90 years of motoring and motorcycling memorabilia.

ISLE OF WIGHT (Map page 40)

Alverstone, nr Sandown. *Riverside Walk Nature Trail.* Off A3056, on the Apse Heath to Alverstone road. Start at the Old Mill in Alverstone.
Arreton. *Arreton Manor.* Furnished early 17th century manor house with wireless, fabric, folk and childhood museums, walk-around dolls' house. Sheep, rabbits and aviary.
Brading. *Wax Museum.*
Brading. *The Roman Villa.* Remains of villa including mosaic pavements and hypocaust.
Brook. *Brook Nature Trail.* Turn off A3055 on to Brook to Calbourne road, and start at Seely Hall, Brook.
Carisbrooke. *Carisbrooke Castle.* Norman

fortress where Charles I was held under house arrest. Working 16th century donkey-wheel.
Chale. *Blackgang Chine.* Includes dinosaur park, adventure-land, smugglers' cave, 'crooked house' and hall of mirrors.
Cowes. *Osborne House.* Country house of Queen Victoria. Apartments remain almost unaltered. Also the *Swiss Cottage* - containing items made and collected by the Royal children.
Havenstreet Station, nr Ryde. *Isle of Wight Steam Railway.* Standard gauge steam rides.
Seaview, nr Ryde. *Flamingo Park Bird Sanctuary.* Various kinds of birds, particularly waterfowl.
Shorwell, nr Newport. *Yafford Mill and Farm Park.* Restored working mill. You can see waterfowl, seals and rare breeds of farm animals. Nature trail.
Yarmouth. *Fort Victoria Country Park Nature Trail.* Take A3054 west of Yarmouth, and turn right along Westhill Lane. Start at Fort Victoria Café.

KENT (Map page 41)

Bekesbourne, nr Canterbury. *Howletts Zoo Park.*
Boughton Monchelsea, nr Maidstone. *Boughton Monchelsea Place.* Elizabethan manor with later alterations. Includes display of dresses, old vehicles and farm implements.
Canterbury. *Canterbury Cathedral.* 6th century.
Chiddingstone, nr Edenbridge. *Chiddingstone Castle.* Contains furniture, pictures, Egyptian collection and Japanese swords.
Deal. *Deal Castle.* Tudor-rose shaped coastal fort built by Henry VIII.
Dover. *Dover Castle.* Stands on an Iron Age burial site. Built from 1180.
Dover. *Dover Lighthouse.* See page 13.
Dover. *Roman Painted House.* Remains of a Roman town house with wall paintings.
Edenbridge. *Hever Castle.* 13th century moated castle with formal, Italian garden, Anne Boleyn exhibition, maze and adventure playground.
Eynsford. *Lullingstone Roman Villa.* With mosaic floor.
Eynsford. *Norman Castle.*
Folkestone. *Eurotunnel Exhibition Centre.* Includes 32m long model railway, floor to ceiling illuminated map, full-sized shuttle interior model, observation tower.
Hythe. *Port Lympne Wildlife Zoo Park, with 20th century mansion.* A wide variety of rare and endangered species.
Hythe-Dungeness. *Romney, Hythe and Dymchurch Railway.* See page 30.
Maidstone. *Leeds Castle.* Furnished castle, built in the middle of a lake in landscaped parkland. Has a museum of medieval dog collars, duckery, maze and secret grotto. Seasonal special events.
Maidstone. *Tyrwhitt-Drake Museum of Carriages.* Horse-drawn vehicles of all types.
Penshurst. *Penshurst Place.* Medieval manor house containing furniture, portraits and armour. Formal terraced garden and vineyard.
Richborough. *Richborough Castle.* Displays of Roman finds from the site.
Rochester. *Rochester Public Museum, Castle and Cathedral. Dickens Centre,* miniature theatre sets and tableaux of life-sized characters.
Sevenoaks. *Knole.* State rooms contain rare furniture, portraits, tapestries, silver, carpets.
Sittingbourne. *Dolphin Yard Sailing Barge Museum.* 'Live' museum with artefacts, barge repairs and sailmaking.
Sittingbourne. *Sittingbourne and Kemsley Light Railway.* Narrow gauge steam rides.
Tenterden. *Kent and East Sussex Railway.* See page 41.

LANCASHIRE (Map page 53)

Blackburn. *Lewis Textile Museum.* Exhibition of early textile machinery.
Blackpool. *Blackpool Zoo.*
Blackpool. *Louis Tussauds.* Waxwork figures of famous people.
Blackpool. *The Sandcastle.* Swimming complex with wave machines, slides etc.
Carnforth. *Leighton Hall.* Dates from 1246, Gothic facade and Victorian wing added later. Antiques include clock collection. Maze, birds of prey.
Carnforth. *Steamtown Railway Museum.* Main line British and continental steam locomotives.
Goosnargh, nr Preston. *Chingle Hall.* Moated

manor house built in 1260.
Helmshore, Rossendale. *Helmshore Textile Museum.* 2 textile mills, a water-wheel and early textile machinery.
Lancaster. *Judges' Lodgings.* Displays of childhood in Lancashire. Doll and toy collection. Victorian schoolroom and nurseries.
Lancaster. *Lancaster Leisure Park.* Includes a children's farmyard, rare breeds unit, wild west fort, adventure playground and go-kart raceway.
Preston. *Harris Museum and Art Gallery.*
Preston. *Hoghton Tower.* 16th century fortified mansion. Exhibition of dolls' houses. Walled gardens.
Ribchester, nr Preston. *Museum of Childhood.* Over 50 dolls' houses, 300 teddy bears, a 20-piece Edwardian fairground and a flea circus.
Ribchester, nr Preston. *The Ribchester Museum.* Remains from the Roman site, and an excavated area showing the granaries.

LEICESTERSHIRE (Map page 48)

Belvoir, nr Grantham. *Belvoir Castle.* See page 48.
Cadeby, nr Market Bosworth. *Cadeby Light Railway, Cadeby Rectory.* Working, narrow gauge railway, model railway and steam museum. Also *Cadeby Brass Rubbing Centre.*
Castle Donington. The *Donington Collection of Single-Seater Racing Cars.* See page 48.
East Midlands Airport. *Aeropark.* Collection of British, French and American aircraft.
Leicester. *The Jewry Wall and Museum of Archaeology.* Foundations of the Roman Baths and collection of prehistoric, Roman, Anglo-Saxon and medieval exhibits.
Leicester. *Museum of Technology, Abbey Pumping Station.* Includes beam engines, steam shovel and horse-drawn vehicles.
Leicester. *Newarke Houses Museum.* Leicester's social history shown by displays of artefacts from 1500, a 17th century room and 19th century street scene.
Loughborough-Leicester. *Great Central Railway.* Britain's only main line steam railway.
Lutterworth. *Stanford Hall.* House contains antiques, pictures and costumes. Nature trail around the park and a walled rose garden. Also a vintage motorcycle collection.
Newton Linford. *Bradgate Park.* Ruins of house and park with large deer population.
Oakham. *Rutland County Museum.* History of the Yeomanry Cavalry, rural life displays, also archaeological finds.
Oakham. *Rutland Farm Park.* Working farm including rare breeds of cattle, ponies, pigs, etc. Also a nature trail.
Sutton Cheney, nr Market Bosworth. *Battlefield of Bosworth Battle Trail.* On the site of the Battle of Bosworth Field 1485. The visitors' centre includes an exhibition and battle models. There is also the *Shackerstone-Market Bosworth Railway* and you can see steam-engines at Shackerstone Station.
Twycross, nr Atherstone. *Twycross Zoo.* See page 30.

LINCOLNSHIRE (Map pages 48 and 51)

Alford. *Alford Windmill.* Six-storey, five-sail tower-mill in working order. Built 1837.
Alford. *Manor House Folk Museum.* Displays include an old sweet factory, 19th century chemist's shop, craftshops, agricultural and transport galleries.
Belton, nr Grantham. *Belton House, Park and Gardens.* Includes paintings, porcelain and tapestries. The park includes woodland and lakeland trails, a miniature railway and carriage and horse museum. Also the *National Cycle Museum.*
Boston. *Boston Guildhall Museum.* You can see prison cells used in 1607 to imprison the Pilgrim Fathers. Also collections of local archaeology.
Doddington, nr Lincoln. *Doddington Hall.* Elizabethan manor including furniture, pictures, textiles and porcelain. The walled gardens include a nature trail.
Gainsborough. *Gainsborough Old Hall.* 15th century manor house with medieval kitchen. Displays of furniture, dolls, period dresses and portraits. Riverside gardens.
Heckington. The only 8-sailed windmill in Great Britain.

Lincoln. *City and County Museum.* History of Lincolnshire from prehistoric times to 1750. Includes replica Roman legion of 6,000 miniature soldiers and a Viking house.
Lincoln. *Lincoln Cathedral.* See page 51.
Lincoln. *Lincoln Castle.* Built by William the Conqueror.
Lincoln. *Lincolnshire Vintage Vehicle Society.* Cars, buses and comercial vehicles, plus old road signs, bus tickets and posters.
Lincoln. *Museum of Lincolnshire Life.*
Mablethorpe. *Mablethorpe's Animal Gardens.*
Skegness. *Church Farm Museum.* 18th century furnished farmhouse and labourer's cottage. Outbuildings house agricultural, industrial and domestic collections.
Skegness. *Gibraltar Point Nature Reserve Nature Trail.* South of Skegness.
Skegness. *Skegness Natureland Marine Zoo.*

LONDON (Map pages 40-41)
See pages 26-29

MERSEYSIDE (Map page 47)

Albert Dock, Liverpool. *Merseyside Maritime Museum.* Floating exhibits, restored buildings, ship models.
Liverpool. *Croxteth Hall and Country Park.* Re-creation of Edwardian life includes craft workshops and walled kitchen garden with Young Growers Club and weather station. Also the *Home Farm.*
Liverpool. *Restoration of Albert Dock Complex.* Largest project of its type in the world.
Liverpool. *Walker Art Gallery.*
Liverpool. *Museum of Labour History.* Working class life on Merseyside from 1840.
Liverpool. *Liverpool Museum.* Diverse and world-wide collections. Also a natural history centre, planetarium and aquarium.
Liverpool. *Speke Hall.* Tudor manor house.
Prescot. *Knowsley Hall and Safari Park.* See page 47.
St Helens. *Pilkington Glass Museum.* History of glass-making techniques.
Southport. *Southport Zoo.*
Southport. *Pleasureland.* Funfair.
Wirral Way. *Country Park.* Nature trails.

NORFOLK (Map page 49)

Aylsham. *Blickling Hall.* Jacobean mansion. Parkland.
Brancaster. *Saxon Shore Fort.*
Brancaster Staithe. *Scolt Head Island.* National nature reserve with nature trail. By boat from Brancaster Staithe harbour, on A149 between Hunstanton and Burnham Market.
Castle Rising. *Norman castle.*
Diss. *Banham Zoo.* Rare and endangered species including primates and big cats. Large collection of owls.
Diss. *Bressingham Live Steam Museum and Gardens.* Steam engines, and narrow gauge railway rides.
East Dereham. *Bishop Bonner's Cottage.* Early 16th century cottage with local history displays.
Felbrigg, nr Cromer. *Felbrigg Hall.* 17th century house with 18th century furniture and pictures. Walled garden, lakeside and woodland walks.
Great Witchingham, nr Norwich. *Norfolk Wildlife Park and Nature Centre.* See page 31.
Great Yarmouth. *Burgh Castle.* Remains of a Roman fort.
Great Yarmouth. *Caister Roman Town.* Remains of a Roman commercial port.
Great Yarmouth. *Maritime Museum.*
King's Lynn. *Museum of Social History.* Life in King's Lynn displayed in an 18th century house.
King's Lynn. *Sandringham House Gardens.* One of the homes of the Queen. Grounds only open, including motor car museum and nature trail.
Norwich. *Bridewell Museum of Local Industries and Rural Crafts.* Local industry from the Middle Ages to the present day, including displays of weaving, leatherwork and clockmaking.
Norwich. *The Mustard Shop.* Colman's Mustard Museum shows how mustard is made.
Norwich. *Norwich Castle.* Contains a museum.
Norwich. *Strangers' Hall Museum of Domestic Life.* Rooms furnished in different periods from 16th to 19th century, plus costumes and textiles.
Sheringham. *North Norfolk Railway Co., Sheringham Station.* See page 49.

Sutton, nr Stalham. *Sutton Windmill.* The tallest mill in the country, with interesting machinery.
Thetford. *Kilverstone Country Park Zoo.* Rare and endangered wildlife, adventure play area. Pets' corner, miniature railway.
Thursford, nr Fakenham. *Thursford Collection of Organs and Engines, Laurel Farm.* Includes steam road engines, mechanical musical organs and a Wurlitzer theatre organ.
Weeton. *Grimes Graves.* See page 49.
West Rudham, between Kings's Lynn and Fakenham. *Houghton Hall.* 18th century house built for the first Prime Minister of England, Sir Robert Walpole. *Soldier Museum* with militaria, 20,000 model soldiers and battlefields. Heavy horses and Shetland ponies in the stables.
Wroxham. *Hoveton Great Broad Nature Trail.* Access by boat only, from Wroxham or Horning.

NORTHAMPTONSHIRE (Map page 48)

Corby. *Rockingham Castle.* See page 48.
Daventry. *Daventry Country Park Nature Trail.* Take B4036 (Welton Road) from Daventry.
Harlestone, nr Northampton. *Althorp.* Originally built in 1508, the house contains a good collection of pictures.
Kettering. *Boughton House.* Tudor monastic building, enlarged mainly in French style. Collections of furniture and pictures, and an armoury. Parkland, woodland and a play area.
Kettering. *Manor House Museum.* Displays of footwear, shoe-making tools and machinery.
Kettering. *Wicksteed Park.* Includes a miniature railway and children's playground.
Little Billing, Northampton. *Billing Mill.* Milling museum housed in a restored corn-grinding mill. You can see the water-wheel and machinery in motion.
Naseby nr Market Harborough. *Museum of Miniature Rural Buildings.* Miniature scale models of castles and rural buildings. Also demonstrations of thatching. You can also visit *Naseby Battle and Farm Museum* which includes a model of Naseby Battlefield, farm tools and old tractors.
Northampton. *Museum of Leathercraft.* Use of leather from Egyptian times until the present. Includes gilt leather, American tribal costumes, saddlery and harnesses.
Oundle. *Southwick Hall.* 14th century manor house with Tudor and 18th century additions.
Stoke Bruerne, nr Northampton. *Canal Museum.* See page 31.

NORTHUMBERLAND (Map page 52)

Alnwick. *Alnwick Castle.* See page 52.
Ashington. *Woodhorn Church Museum.* Monthly exhibitions.
Bamburgh. *Bamburgh Castle.*
Cambo. *Wallington Hall.* Collections of porcelain, needlework, dolls' houses and dolls.
Chillingham, nr Wooler. *Chillingham Wild White Cattle.* Herd of pure wild white cattle which have roamed the area for 700 years. Also, *Chillingham Castle.*
Farne Islands. See page 52.
Ford. *Heatherslaw Mill.* Restored working water-mill and agricultural museum.
Glanton. *Bird Field Study Museum.* Britain's first bird research station. 7 exhibition rooms.
Hadrian's Wall. See page 13. Today, not all of the Wall is visible. Some of the important sites are:
  Bardon Mill. *Vindolanda.* Remains of main garrison fort plus full-size reconstruction of a stone turret and a wooden gate tower. The museum in *Chesterholm Country House* includes articles from everyday Roman life found at the site.
  Chesters, nr Chollerford. The best preserved Roman cavalry fort in Britain. Also *The Clayton Collection* of archaeological finds.
  Corbridge. *Corbridge Roman Station.* See page 52.
  Housesteads. *Roman garrison remains.* Includes granaries, commandant's house, barrack blocks, latrines and gateways.
Holy Island. *Lindisfarne Castle.* Tudor fort converted into a private home in 1903. Includes oak furniture and a collection of prints. Accessible at low tide by causeway.
Holy Island. *Lindisfarne Priory.* Founded AD635

and thought to be the birthplace of Christianity in Britain. Contains Anglo-Saxon sculpture, medieval pottery and reproductions of the Lindisfarne gospels.
Kielder Water. One of Britain's largest man-made lakes, in the Border forest. Most forms of watersports and outdoor activities.
Morpeth. *Bagpipe Museum.*
Rothbury. *Cragside.* First house in the world to be lit by hydro-electric power. Restored to 1860s. Pre-Raphaelite pictures and experimental scientific apparatus.
Seaton Sluice. *Seaton Delaval Hall.* House, designed by Vanbrugh, completed in 1732. Stables and gardens.

NORTH YORKSHIRE (Map pages 50-51 and 53)

Aldborough. *The Aldborough Roman Museum.* Roman pottery, glass, coins and metalwork.
Aysgarth Falls. *The Yorkshire Museum of Carriages and Horse-Drawn Vehicles.*
Boroughbridge. *The Devil's Arrows.* See page 51.
Clapham, nr Settle. *Ingleborough Cave.* Show cave with stalactites, stalagmites, etc.
Embsay, nr Skipton. *Yorkshire Dales Steam Railway.*
Grosmont-Pickering. *North York Moors Railway.* Steam rides through the National Park.
Hawes. *Dales Countryside Museum.* Traditional trades and occupations, including displays of hay and sheep-farming, peat-cutting, hand-knitting, cheese-making.
Helmsley. *Rievaulx Abbey.* Cistercian monastery ruins. Visitors' centre with display telling the story of the monastery.
Hutton-le-Hole. *Ryedale Folk Museum.* Prehistoric and Roman antiquities, 19th century craft tools, domestic equipment and other displays. In the *Folk Park* are old buildings including a blacksmith's furnace and a 16th century manor house.
Ingleton. *White Scar Caves.* Limestone caves with stalactites, stalagmites and waterfalls. Nearby is a waterfall walk.
Kirby Misperton, nr Malton. *Flamingoland.* Zoo of over 1,000 animals, including a children's farm and animal shows. Also a fun park with over 100 rides.
Knaresborough. *Mother Shipton's Cave, Dropping Well Estate.* See page 30.
Malton. *Castle Howard.* See page 50.
Pateley Bridge. *Stump Cross Caverns.* Stalactites and stalagmites in floodlit caves.
Pickering. *Beck Isle Museum of Rural Life.*
Pickering. *Dalby Forest Visitor Centre, Low Dalby.* Forest walks, displays, and films.
Richmond. *Georgian Theatre Royal.* Built in 1788, the country's oldest theatre still in its original form. Productions throughout the year. Also a theatre museum.
Richmond. *Richmond Castle.* See page 50.
Ripley. *Ripley Castle.* Medieval collection in the 1555 tower. Royal Greenwich armour and secret priest's hiding hole. Garden, lake and deer park.
Ripon. *Fountains Abbey.* See page 50.
Ripon. *Newby Hall.* Adam house containing tapestries and sculptures. Miniature riverside railway, adventure gardens and rock garden with waterfalls. Woodland discovery walk and picnic areas.
Snaith, nr Selby. *Carlton Towers.* Contains furniture, silver, china, pictures. There is also a priest's hiding hole. Railway exhibition.
York. *Beningbrough Hall.* Built about 1716, contains 100 portraits from the *National Portrait Gallery.* Victorian laundry with domestic life exhibition. Wilderness play area, pike ponds, riverside walk.
York. *Jorvik Viking Centre.* 'Time car journey' to a re-created Viking city next to the archaeological dig. Display of finds.
York. *The Museum of Automata.* Collection of machines spanning 2,000 years.
York. *National Railway Museum.* See page 31.
York. *York Castle Museum.* Folk museum of Yorkshire life including period rooms, cobbled streets of shops, early crafts, toys, domestic and agricultural equipment.
York. *York Model Railway Co.* Large model railway layout.
York. *The York Story.* A history of the city from Roman times shown in models, reconstructions, audio-visual displays and artefacts.

NOTTINGHAMSHIRE (Map pages 48 and 51)

Creswell, nr Worksop. *Creswell Crags Picnic Site and Visitors' Centre.* Limestone caves and gorge. The visitors' centre has displays of archaeological finds depicting life of Stone Age man.

Edwinstowe, nr Mansfield. *Sherwood Forest Country Park and Visitors' Centre.* Audio-visual show in the visitors' centre. See the Major Oak in the forest, where Robin Hood and his Merry Men used to meet.

Limby. *Newstead Abbey.* Contains possessions of the poet Byron, including pictures and furniture. In the park are lakes, waterfalls and different types of garden.

Newark-on-Trent. *Newark Air Museum.* Displays of aircraft and aircraft parts, including engines and propellers. Also model aircraft.

Nottingham. *Museum of Costume and Textiles.* Displays include the history of lace, textiles, costumes and embroideries, dolls' clothes.

Nottingham. *Nottingham Castle.* Built in the 17th century. Now houses *City Museum.*

Nottingham. *Nottingham Industrial Museum, Wollaton Hall.* Housed in the 18th century stables, the displays tell the stories of Nottingham's industries - printing, hosiery, lace-making, and pharmacy.

Nottingham. *Wollaton Hall and Natural History Museum.* Elizabethan house, with collections of rocks, plants and animals. The gardens include a deer park and lakeside nature trail.

Worksop. *Clumber Park and Chapel.*

OXFORDSHIRE (Map pages 40 and 48)

Banbury. *Broughton Castle.* Built in 1300, with Tudor additions. Contents include furniture and arms and armour.

Burford. *Cotswold Wildlife Park.* Wide variety of wildlife from around the world. Includes an animal brass-rubbing centre, adventure playground and miniature railway.

Burford. *Tolsey Museum.* Illustrates the effect of England's history on a small country town.

Cogges, nr Witney. *Manor Farm Museum.* Edwardian farm, including kitchens, dairy and animals. Also nature trail and historic trail.

Combe, nr Woodstock. *Combe Mill.* Sawmill built in 1852, includes a working beam engine. You can also see a blacksmith at work.

Didcot. *Didcot Railway Centre.* Great Western Railway steam-engines in original engine shed. Steam train rides.

Henley-on-Thames. *Greys Court.* Jacobean house with Georgian additions in the remains of a 14th century fortified house. Early Tudor, donkey-wheel, well-house and Archbishop's Maze.

Henley-on-Thames. *Stonor Park.* Built over many centuries, includes furniture, portraits, stained glass and Italian sculpture. Wooded deer park.

Oxford. *The Ashmolean Museum of Art and Archaeology.* Collections include archaeology, paintings, ceramics, sculpture and silver.

Oxford. *Museum of the History of Science.* Includes early scientific instruments such as astrolabes, microscopes, medical and photographic equipment. Also clocks.

Oxford. *University Botanic Gardens.*

Mapledurham, nr Reading (Berks). *Mapledurham House.* See page 40.

Steeple Aston. *Rousham House.* 17th century house containing furniture and portraits. In the gardens are waterfalls and statues.

Witney. *North Leigh.* Remains of a Roman building laid out round a courtyard, including a mosaic pavement.

Woodstock. *Blenheim Palace.* See page 18. You can see pictures, tapestries and a Churchill exhibition. There are gardens, boat trips on the lake and a narrow gauge steam railway.

SCILLY ISLES (Map page 42)

St Mary's. *Porth Hellick Down.* Group of five tombs, either Stone Age or Bronze Age.

St Mary's. *St Mary's Museum.* Natural history, archaeology and geology of the Isles, plus treasure from ancient shipwrecks.

Tresco. *Cromwell's Castle.* Round Tower dating from the 17th century.

Tresco. *Tresco Abbey.* Sub-tropical gardens including palms and yuccas.

Tresco. *Valhalla Maritime Museum.* Includes figure-heads and ships' ornaments, salvaged from ships wrecked in the area.

SHROPSHIRE (Map pages 45 and 47)

Acton Scott, nr Church Stretton. *Acton Scott Working Farm Museum.* Working farm using heavy horses, demonstrating 19th century farming techniques and traditional crafts. You can see various old breeds of animals.

Bridgnorth. *Midland Motor Museum.* More than 55 vehicles, including sports cars and motor cycles.

Bridgnorth. *Severn Valley Railway.* 20km steam train ride along River Trent to Bewdley and Kidderminster.

Burwarton, Cleobury North. *Brown Clee Nature Trail.* B4364 to Cleobury North. Burwarton is about 1½km west of Cleobury North.

Craven Arms. *Stokesay Castle.* See page 45.

Ironbridge, Telford. *Ironbridge Gorge Museum.* See page 31.

Ludlow. *Ludlow Castle.*

Old Coleham, Shrewsbury. *Coleham Pumping Station.* Preserved beam engines.

Shifnal. *Weston Park.* See page 47.

SOMERSET (Map page 43)

Cheddar. *Cheddar Caves Museum and Exhibition.* Coloured caverns with 9,000 year-old skeleton. Children's play cave and Crystal Quest fantasy adventure. Museum and exhibition. Cheddar Gorge views.

Cloutsham, Porlock. *Cloutsham Woodland Trail.* Circular trail starting at Webber's Post car park, Dunkery Beacon, to the south of Porlock.

Cranmore, nr Shepton Mallet. *East Somerset Railway, Cranmore Station.* Standard gauge steam railway.

Cricket St Thomas, nr Chard. *The West Country Wildlife and Leisure Park.* Wide variety of birds and animals, many roaming free. Heavy horse centre, rare breeds and children's farm. Adventure playgrounds and craft centre.

Glastonbury. *Glastonbury Abbey.*

Glastonbury. *Somerset Rural Life Museum.* Late 19th century farm with horse-drawn agricultural machinery and vehicles, wheelwright's workshop, cider-making, withy-cutting and Cheddar cheese displays.

Minehead-Bishop's Lydeard. *West Somerset Railway.* 32km of track. Diesel rides all year round, steam train rides in the summer.

Montacute. *Montacute House.* See page 43.

Street. *The Shoe Museum.* Displays of the history of shoemaking including shoes from Roman times.

Washford Station, nr Watchet. *Somerset and Dorset Railway Trust.* Short steam rides.

Wells. *Wells Cathedral.* Also *Bishop's Palace and Moat.*

Wookey Hole. *Wookey Hole Caves.* See page 43.

Yeovilton. *Fleet Air Arm Museum.* See page 43.

SOUTH YORKSHIRE (Map page 51)

Cawthorne. *Cannon Hall.* A country house museum displaying furniture, glass, and paintings. Also a regimental museum.

Rotherham. *Clifton Park Museum.* 18th century furnished rooms and period kitchen. Also displays of Victoriana, glass and glass-making equipment, local natural history, etc.

Rotherham. *Conisbrough Castle.* See page 51.

Sheffield. *Abbeydale Industrial Hamlet.* See page 47. Also *Kelham Island Industrial Museum.*

Sheffield. *Rivelin Nature Trail.* Rails Road, Western Sheffield. Take the A57 or A6101.

Sheffield. *South Yorkshire Fire Service Museum.* In the Victorian West Bar Police/Fire Station. Includes old fire-engines, uniforms and equipment, safety displays, memorabilia. Play area has miniature pole and fire-engine.

Worsbrough, nr Barnsley. *Worsbrough Mill Museum.* Country park setting for a working industrial museum.

STAFFORDSHIRE (Map page 47)

Alton, nr Cheadle. *Alton Towers.* Once Europe's largest privately-owned family home, now a theme park with over 125 attractions in 500 acres of landscaped gardens.

Barlaston, Stoke-on-Trent. *Josiah Wedgwood & Sons Ltd.* Visitors' centre includes a craft demonstration area, museum and galleries.

Brownhills. *Chasewater Railway, Chasewater Steam Park.* Locomotives and rolling stock dating from 1875 to 1975. Other railway relics.

Burton-on-Trent. *Bass Museum of Brewing.* See page 48.

Cheddleton, nr Leek. *Cheddleton Flint Mill.* Working, restored water-mill with two large wheels.

Cheddleton, nr Leek. *Cheddleton Railway Centre.* Steam locomotives, coaches, memorabilia etc.

Codsall, nr Wolverhampton. *Codsall Nature Trail.* Take A41 west from Wolverhampton, turn right after 'Crown' at Wergs. Trail starts in Oaken Lanes just before Codsall village.

Dilhorne, nr Cheadle. *Foxfield Steam Railway.* Steam train return trip from Blythe Bridge.

Fenton, Stoke-on-Trent. *Coalport Minerva Works.* 1½ hour tour, from making to final firing of chinaware and florals.

Hanley, Stoke-on-Trent. *Spitfire Museum.*

Hoar Cross, nr Burton-on-Trent. *Hoar Cross Hall.* Includes European armour, Victorian furnishings, pictures and costumes.

Lichfield. *Hanch Hall.* Built in the 13th century, with later additions. Collections of teapots, dolls, shells, needlework and costumes.

Longton, Stoke-on-Trent. Gladstone Pottery Museum. See page 31.

Shugborough, Stafford. *Staffordshire County Museum and Mansion House.* House has 18th century furniture, pictures and silver. The museum has a brewhouse, coach-houses, laundry and working kitchen. At *Shugborough Park Farm* you can see a working cornmill, dairy, bread ovens and rare breed centre.

Tamworth. *Drayton Manor Park and Zoo.*

Tamworth. *Tamworth Castle and Museum.* 12th century keep and tower, with later additions. Norman exhibition with 'speaking knight'.

Wall, nr Lichfield. *Wall Roman Site.* Remains of Letocetum posting station and baths. Finds from the excavation are displayed in museum.

SUFFOLK (Map page 49)

Bury St Edmunds. *Ickworth.* Built 1795-1829. Contains furniture, silver and pictures. Orangery, children's playground, deer enclosure, lake and woodland walks.

Earsham, nr Bungay. *Otter Trust.* See page 31.

Framlingham. *Framlingham Castle.* See page 15.

Helmingham, nr Debenham. *Helmingham Hall Gardens.* Moated Elizabethan gardens, including Highland cattle and safari ride in the deer park.

Ipswich. *Christchurch.* Tudor house and garden. Also *Wolsey Art Gallery* and a Victorian toy collection.

Ipswich. *Ipswich Museum and Art Gallery.* Includes replicas of the Sutton Hoo Saxon treasure hoard and the Mildenhall Roman silver treasure.

Kessingland, nr Lowestoft. *Suffolk Wildlife Park.*

Lavenham. *Guildhall.* Box-framed, 16th century building, displaying the history of the wool industry.

Lowestoft. *Maritime Museum.* Models of boats, plus shipwrights' tools, etc.

Lowestoft. *Somerleyton Hall.* State rooms include paintings and carvings. In the gardens are a maze, garden trail and miniature railway.

Orford. *Orford Castle.* Has an 18-sided keep.

Saxtead Green, nr Framlingham. *Saxtead Green Windmill.* 18th century, 3-storey, post-mill, restored to perfect condition.

Sudbury. *Gainsborough's House.* Gainsborough's birthplace including some of his possessions, and a collection of his paintings.

West Stow, nr Bury St Edmunds. *West Stow Anglo-Saxon Village.* Hall and houses constructed by Anglo-Saxon methods and materials. Nature trail and children's playground.

Woodbridge. *Woodbridge Tide Mill.* Restored, working water-mill built in 1793.

SURREY (Map pages 40-41)

Chessington. *Chessington World of Adventures.* Over 100 rides and attractions, including a circus and zoo.

Dorking. *Polesden Lacey.* 1820s Regency villa with collections of furniture, tapestries and pictures. Grounds include a walled rose garden. Summer open-air plays.

Esher. *Claremont Landscape Garden.* Includes a lake with an island and pavilion, a grotto and a turf amphitheatre.

Ewell. *Bourne Hall Museum.* Varied collection includes dolls, costumes and toys.

Farnham. *Old Kiln Agricultural Museum.* Open-air collections of farm implements, machines, waggons. Wheelwrights and working smithy.

Godalming. *Winkworth Arboretum.* Wide variety of trees and shrubs and two lakes.

Guildford. *Modern Cathedral.*

Guildford. *Guildford Museum.* Exhibits illustrating the work of the local glass and iron industries. Items from the Surrey Iron Railway, archaeological finds and a needlework collection.

Guildford. *Loseley House.* Elizabethan mansion including panelling, fine ceilings, furniture, tapestries and needlework.

Haslemere. *Educational Museum.* Displays of British birds, zoology, botany, geology and local industries.

Holt Pond, nr Farnham. *Birdworld Zoological Gardens.*

West Clandon, nr Guildford. *Clandon Park.* 18th century, Classical style, furnished house with a military museum.

TYNE & WEAR (Map page 50)

Newcastle. *Hancock Museum.* Natural history displays including fossils, birds, a Mummy Room and Abel's Ark.

Newcastle. *Museum of Antiquities.* Prehistoric, Roman, Anglo-Saxon and medieval displays.

Newcastle. *Science Museum.* Exhibits ranging from shipbuilding, engineering and transport to mining and electricity. Also *Science Factory* with hands-on devices.

St Mary's Island, Whitley Bay. *St Mary's Island Nature Trail.* On A193, north of Whitley Bay. Watch out for the lighthouse and signposts, and start at car park by Curry's Point.

South Shields. *Arbeia Roman Fort Museum.* Objects found at the site of the Roman Fort.

Springwell, nr Gateshead. *Bowes Railway.* Standard gauge steam-engines.

Sunderland. *Monkwearmouth Station Museum.* 1848 station with restored, original booking office.

Sunderland. *Ryhope Engines Museum.* Water-pumping station with two 1868 beam engines, which are run under steam power.

Washington. *Washington Old Hall.* Jacobean manor house. Ancestral home of George Washington, first President of the USA. Built 1183.

Washington. *Washington Wildfowl Refuge.* See page 50.

WARWICKSHIRE (Map page 48)

Alcester. *Ragley Hall.* See page 48.

Kenilworth. *Kenilworth Castle.* Built in 1120.

Kenilworth. *Stoneleigh Abbey.* Abbey and park, gardens and woodlands.

Nuneaton. *Arbury Hall.* Elizabethan and 18th century, Gothic house and gardens. Displays of veteran cycles.

Shottery, nr Stratford-upon-Avon. *Anne Hathaway's Cottage.*

Stratford-upon-Avon. *Hall's Croft.* Furnished Tudor house with walled garden.

Stratford-upon-Avon. *Royal Shakespeare Theatre Picture Gallery and Museum.*

Stratford-upon-Avon. *Shakespeare's Birthplace.* Box-framed house with Shakespeare exhibits.

near Tamworth. *Kingsbury Water Park.* 20 little lakes linked by footpaths. Many kinds of watersports. Nature reserve with trails and hides. Also an adventure playground.

Warwick. *Baddesley Clinton.* Medieval, moated house. Great Hall, formal garden and priest's hiding hole.

Warwick. *Warwick Castle.* 11th century castle, including dungeons, torture chamber, ghost tower, armoury and Tussauds waxworks.

Warwick. *Warwick Doll Museum, Oken's House.*

Wilmcote, nr Stratford-upon-Avon. *Mary Arden's House.* Tudor farmhouse with farm museum.

WEST MIDLANDS (Map pages 45 and 48)

Bagington, nr Coventry. *Lunt Roman Fort.* See page 13.

Bagington, nr Coventry. *Midland Air Museum.* Military aircraft.

Birmingham. *Birmingham Botanical Gardens.* Gardens with greenhouses of tropical and other plants. Tropical and other birds, pets' corner and play area.

Birmingham. *Birmingham Museum of Science and Industry.* Engineering, locomotive, transport and aircraft displays, including several press-button exhibits.

Birmingham. *Birmingham Nature Centre.* British and European mammals, birds and reptiles. Walk-through aviary.

Birmingham. *Birmingham Railway Museum.* Collection of standard gauge steam-engines.

Birmingham. *Sarehole Mill.* 18th century water-powered corn mill. One wheel is working, and there is a display of milling items.

Coventry. *Coventry Cathedral.* Linked to the ruins of the old cathedral, destroyed during the longest air raid on a single British city in World War II.

Coventry. *Coventry Toy Museum.* 6,000 toys dating back to 1760, including dolls, trains, games and amusement machines.

Dudley. *Black Country Museum.* Open-air museum recreates the industrial past of the Midlands. Restored village, colliery, ironworks and fairground with electric tram rides and canal trips.

Dudley. *Dudley Zoo.* See page 45.

West Bromwich. *Oak House.* Tudor house with panelled rooms and oak furniture.

WEST SUSSEX (Map pages 40-41)

Arundel. *Arundel Castle.* Built in Norman times, restored in 18th and 19th centuries. Includes armour, furniture, picture gallery and extensive library.

Arundel. *Arundel Wildfowl & Wetlands Trust.* Includes black swans and tree-nesting ducks.

Bignor. *Bignor Roman Villa.* Remains include mosaics, jewellery, pottery, and a hypocaust.

Bramber. *St Mary's.* 15th century box-framed house, with Elizabethan painted room and animal topiary.

Charlwood. *Gatwick Zoo.*

Chichester. *Weald and Downland Open-Air Museum.* See page 31.

Fishbourne, Chichester. *The Roman Palace.* See pages 13 and 40.

Goodwood. *Goodwood House.* Contains furniture, tapestries, porcelain and pictures.

Henfield. *Woods Mill Nature Trail.* On A2037, start at the water-mill.

Horsham. *Horsham Museum.* Reconstructed craft workshops and barn, Victorian kitchen, transport gallery, ceramics, toys and costumes.

Petworth. *Petworth House.* Fine collection of paintings, including some by Turner, who painted here. Gardens and deer park.

Portfield. *Chichester Mechanical Music and Dolls Collection.*

Pulborough. *Parham.* Elizabethan house including a long gallery. Contains furniture, armour, tapestries and needlework. Deer park.

West Stoke, Chichester. *Kingley Vale National Nature Reserve Nature Trail.* West Stoke is 5½km north east of Chichester. Car park near church, then walk north on footpath for 1km to southern edge of the reserve.

WEST YORKSHIRE (Map pages 47, 51 and 53)

Aberford, nr Leeds. *Lotherton Hall.* Edwardian house. Contains pictures, silver, furniture, porcelain and costumes. Bird garden and deer park.

Bradford. *Bolling Hall.* Manor house with rooms furnished in 17th and 18th century styles.

Bradford. *Industrial Museum.* Includes displays of local industries, mill manager's house, workers' cottages, Victorian stable of shire horses and a horse-drawn tram.

Halifax. *Eureka!* Children's museum with hands-on displays about the body and the world around us.

Halifax. *West Yorkshire Folk Museum, Shibden Hall.* 1420 box-framed house containing 17th century furniture. Also displays of coaches,

harnesses, early agricultural equipment and craft workshops. Park.

Haworth. *Brontë Parsonage.* See page 53.

Hebden Bridge. *Heptonstall Old Grammar School Museum.* Contains 17th century school furniture and local farm and domestic items.

Ilkley. *Ilkley Moor Nature Trail and Ilkley Moor Geology trail.*

Keighley. *Worth Valley Railway.* Standard gauge steam train rides.

Kirkstall. *Kirkstall Abbey Museum.* See page 51.

Leeds. *Harewood House and Bird Garden.* See pages 18 and 51.

Leeds. *Middleton Railway Trust.* Standard gauge steam and diesel engines. Steam rides.

Wakefield. *Nostell Priory.* 18th century house containing furniture and pictures. Rose garden, lakeside walk, adventure playground and craft centre.

Wetherby. *Bramham Park.* Queen Anne mansion with gardens laid out in 18th century French formal design.

WILTSHIRE (Map pages 40 and 43)

Amesbury. *Stonehenge.* See page 12.

Avebury. *Avebury Henge.* See page 45.

Beckhampton. *Silbury Hill.* Prehistoric man-made mound 40m high, the largest in Europe.

Brokerswood, nr Westbury. *The Woodland Park Trails.* Various walks. Leave A36 at Standerwick, and go through Rudge to reach Brokerswood.

Calne. *Bowood.* Exhibition rooms include costumes, furniture, sculpture and water colours. Lake, arboretum and adventure playground.

Lacock, nr Chippenham. *Fox Talbot Museum.* Photography museum.

Lacock, nr Chippenham. *Lacock Abbey.* 13th century abbey converted into a house in 1540. A Gothic hall built in 1754.

Salisbury. *Old Sarum.* Earliest remains are Iron Age, but most of the visible parts are Norman.

Salisbury. *Salisbury and South Wiltshire Museum.*

Salisbury. *Wilton House.* Tudor kitchen and dolls' house exhibition. Adventure playground and gardens.

Stourhead. *House and gardens.* Country house built in 1721.

Swindon. *Great Western Railway Museum.* Great Western Railway engines and models, nameplates, posters, tickets. Room devoted to Brunel, also restored railwayman's cottage.

Warminster. *The Lions of Longleat, Longleat Park.* See page 18.

West Kennet. *West Kennet Long Barrow.* Well-preserved Stone Age burial chamber.

Wroughton, nr Swindon. *Barbury Castle.* Iron Age hill fort.

WALES

CLWYD (Map pages 46-47)

Chirk, nr Llangollen. *Chirk Castle.* Built 1310 by Edward I. Contains portraits, armour and a 4-poster bed. Gardens.

Colwyn Bay. *Dinosaur World.* Over 40 life-size dinosaur models with sound effects. 'Dinosaur' play area.

Colwyn Bay. *The Welsh Mountain Zoo and Botanic Gardens.*

Denbigh. *Denbigh Castle.* Begun in 1282.

Llangollen. *The Canal Exhibition Centre.* Tells story of canals using working and static models. Canal trips.

Llangollen. *Plas Newydd Museum.*

Llangollen. *Valle Crucis Abbey.* Ruins of a 13th century abbey and chapter house. Exhibition on the life of Cistercian monks.

Rhos-on-Sea, Colwyn Bay. *Harlequin Puppet Theatre.* On the Promenade.

Rhyl. *Sun Centre* - Indoor leisure complex with swimming pools and surfing pool, wave machines, indoor monorail, and enormous dragon slide.

St Asaph, nr Rhyl. *Bodelwyddan Castle.* Large collection of portraits, furniture and sculptures. Adventure woodland. Also *The Discovery Dome* hands-on science centre and technology workshop.

St Asaph, nr Rhyl. *St Asaph Cathedral.* One of the smallest of the ancient cathedrals in Britain. Founded AD 560 but much altered due to

damage during the Civil War.
Wrexham. *Erddig Hall.* See page 47.

DYFED (Map page 44)

Aberaeron. *Aberaeron Aquarium.*
Aberystwyth. *Aberystwyth Cliff Railway.* Electric railway to the top of Constitution Hill.
Aberystwyth-Devil's Bridge. *Vale of Rheidol Railway.* See page 44.
Bronwydd Arms Station, nr Carmarthen. *Gwili Steam Railway.* Standard gauge steam train rides.
Llandysul. *Maesllyn Woollen Mill Museum.* Working mill museum with weaving demonstrations. Also vintage wireless collection and nature trails in grounds.
Llandysul. *Museum of the Welsh Woollen Industry.* History of the woollen industry from the Middle Ages onwards. Shows the process of fleece to fabric. Also a working mill.
Newport. *Pentre Ifan Cromlech.* See page 44.
Ponterwyd, nr Aberystwyth. *Llywernog Silver-Lead Mine.* Restored, water-powered silver-lead mine with a floodlit underground tunnel.
Tenby. *Manor House Wildlife and Leisure Park.* Aquarium, pets' corner and model railway.
Trevine. *Carreg Samson Cromlech.* Stone Age burial chamber.

GWENT (Map page 45)

Abercarn, nr Newport. *Cwmcarn Scenic Forest Drive.* Drive through forest, which has adventure play areas, picnic areas and walks.
Abergavenny. *Abergavenny and District Museum, The Castle.* Displays of local archaeology, rural crafts and a turn of century Welsh kitchen.
Abergavenny. *Museum of Childhood.*
Blaenavon. *Big Pit.* Preserved coalmine.
Caerleon. *Roman Amphitheatre.* See page 13. Also, the *Legionary Museum,* which has displays of finds from the Roman site.
Caerwent. *Caerwent Roman Site and Walls.* You can see the gateways, the remains of houses and a forge from the old Roman town.
Caldicot. *Caldicot Castle Museum.* One tower with furnished rooms, a second tower with exhibitions. Costume gallery. Cellar with display of castle artefacts.
Chepstow. *Chepstow Castle.* Begun before 1071. Exhibition on the castle through the ages. Life-size models of the medieval lords and a Civil War battle scene.
Llangwm, nr Chepstow. *Wolvesnewton Folk Museum.* Domestic and agricultural items.
Newport. *Tredegar House and Park.* 17th century house. In the grounds are a children's adventure play-farm, boating lake and craft workshops.
Raglan. *Raglan Castle.* 15th century moated castle.
Tintern. *The Old Station.* Restored Victorian country station, visitors' centre and picnic site.

GWYNEDD (Map page 46)

Bala. *Sporting Centre,* for sailing, fishing, golf, pony-trekking and walking.
Bangor. *Bangor Art Gallery and Museum of Welsh Antiquities.*
Blaenau Ffestiniog. *Llechwedd Slate Caverns.* Tramway rides through the mine workings, and demonstrations by quarrymen. Restored Victorian village and working smithy.
Caernarfon. *Segontium Roman Fort Museum.* Foundations of the fort can be seen.
Conwy. *Conwy Castle.* See page 46.
Fairbourne. *The Fairbourne and Barmouth Steam Railway.* Only 31cm wide. 4½ km journey.
Great Ormes Head. *Great Orme Nature Trail.* Guided walk, but you can break off earlier and return by tram or cablecar.
Isle of Anglesey. *Beaumaris Gaol.* Old Victorian gaol.
Llanbedr. *Cefn Isa Farm Trail.* 2½km long. Turn inland off A496 at Llanbedr, follow signs to Cwm Bychan and Cwm Nantcol. Trail is 90m beyond Salem chapel.
Llanbedr. *Maes Artro Village.* Recreated old Welsh street. Sea-life aquarium, RAF museum with full-size replica Spitfire, adventure playground, rural exhibition.
Llanberis. *Llanberis Lake Railway.* 3km trip

along Llyn Padarn to Penllyn, and back. Nature trail.
Llanberis. *Museum of the North.* Exhibition gallery, natural science theatre and 'The Power of Wales' display. Trips into the *Dinorwig Power Station.*
Llanberis. *Welsh Slate Museum.* Machinery and equipment depicting the local slate-quarrying industry. Also the biggest working iron water-wheel in the world.
Llanberis-Snowdon Summit. *Snowdon Mountain Railway.* 2½ hour round trip.
Llandudno. *Childhood Revisited.* See page 31.
Llanfairpwll, Isle of Anglesey. *Plas Newydd.* 18th century house by Menai Strait. Has a military museum. Large wall mural. Garden.
Llanuwchylln-Bala. *Bala Lake Railway.* Runs along Bala Lake, the largest in Wales.
Menai Bridge. *Museum of Childhood.* See page 46.
Porthmadog-Tanygrisiau. *Ffestiniog Railway.* Plus Ffestiniog Railway Museum.
Portmeirion. *Private village,* where each house is built in a different Italian architectural style. Also *Gwyllt Gardens* which include woodland walks.
Tywyn. *The Narrow Gauge Railway Museum.*
Tywyn-Nant Gwernol. *Talyllyn Railway.*

MID GLAMORGAN (Map pages 44-45)

Aberdare. *Dare Valley.* Moorland including ponds and waterfalls. You can follow an Industrial Trail, telling the development of coalmining in the area. Playground and picnic areas.
Caerphilly. *Caerphilly Castle.* See page 44.
Porthcawl. *Coney Beach Amusement Park and Pleasure Beach.* Model village, dinosaur park, rides, games and sideshows.

POWYS (Map pages 44-45 and 46-47)

Abercrave. *Dan-yr-Ogof Caves.* See page 44.
Crickhowell. *Tretower Court and Castle.* Late medieval defended house with earlier castle stronghold.
Llandrindod Wells. *Castle Collen.* Site of a former Roman fort.
Llandrindod Wells. *Llandrindod Wells Museum.* Doll collection and history of Llandrindod Wells.
The Automobile Palace, Llandrindod Wells. *Tom Norton's Collection of Old Cycles and Tricycles.*
Llanfair Caereinion. *Welshpool and Llanfair Light Railway.* Journey through open countryside.
Llanidloes. *Hafren Cascades.* Forest area including waterfalls and nature trails.
Machynlleth. *Centre for Alternative Technology.* Working demonstrations, set in an old slate quarry, of solar-, water- and wind-powered machinery, energy conservation, organic gardening etc.
Newtown. *Textile Museum.* Housed in an old handloom weaving factory, the collections include machinery, handlooms and costumes.
Welshpool. *Powis Castle.*
Welshpool. *Powysland Museum.* 19th century shop fronts and the story of wool and archaeological material. Also *The Montgomery Canal Centre* with canal artefacts.

SOUTH GLAMORGAN (map pages 44-45)

Barry Island. *Porthkerry Park.* Beach and wooded valley containing woodland trails, picnic areas, miniature golf etc.
Cardiff. *Castell Coch.* 13th century foundations with Victorian reconstruction in Gothic style. Ornate painted rooms.
Cardiff. *The National Museum of Wales.* Story of Wales in six departments - plants, rocks, animals, archaeology, art and industry. Holiday activities for children.
Cardiff. *Welsh Folk Museum, St Fagans Castle.* See page 45.
Cardiff. *Welsh Industrial and Maritime Museum.*
Tinkinswood. *Stone Age Burial Chamber.*

WEST GLAMORGAN (Map page 44)

Aberavon, nr Port Talbot. *Aberavon Promenade and Afan Lido.* Includes a funfair, sports hall, boating, swimming and paddling pools.
Afan Argoes, nr Port Talbot. *Afan Argoed*

Country Park. Includes nature walks, a picnic area, cycle hire and mountain bike tracks. Also *The Welsh Miners Museum* with coal mining industry in South Wales, including replicas of the coal-face and a miner's cottage.
Clifrew, nr Neath. *Penscynor Wildlife Park.* See page 44.
Knelston. *Gower Farm Trail.* Various lengths. From *Gower Farm Museum.*
Port Talbot. *Margam Park.* Includes nursery rhyme village, hedge maze, road train, farm trail, giant chess and draughts, putting and live children's entertainers.
Rhosili. *Gower Coast Trail.* From the church at Rhosili to LLangennith.
Swansea. *Maritime and Industrial Museum.*

SCOTLAND

BORDERS (Map page 52)

Dryburgh, nr Melrose. *Dryburgh Abbey.* Ruins of 12th century abbey.
Hawick. *Hawick Museum and Art Gallery.* Geology, natural history, local history, coins and medals. In *Wilton Lodge Park,* which has gardens and riverside walks.
Hermitage, nr Newcastleton. *Hermitage Castle.* 14th century fortress at the centre of much of the turbulent border history. Connected with Mary Queen of Scots.
Innerleithen. *Traquair House.* Mansion dating from 10th century, containing embroideries, glass, pictures, books, an 18th century library and a secret staircase. There is a working 18th century brewhouse, craft workshops, a maze and woodland walks.
Jedburgh. *Castle Jail Museum.* Reconstructed rooms from early 19th century prison.
Jedburgh. *Jedburgh Abbey.* See page 52.
Jedburgh. *Mary Queen of Scots' House.* Museum containing relics associated with Mary Queen of Scots.
Kelso. *Kelso Abbey.* Ruins of 12th century abbey.
Mellerstain, nr Kelso. *Mellerstain House.* Furnished, 18th century, Adam mansion. Terraced gardens and lake in grounds.
Melrose. *Abbotsford House.* Home of novelist Sir Walter Scott, with his collection of historic relics, armouries and huge library.
Melrose. *Melrose Abbey.* 14th-16th century remains of a Gothic abbey.
Peebles. *Neidpath Castle.* 14th century castle, built on a hill above the River Tweed. Good views.
Selkirk. *Bowhill.* 19th century house with paintings, furniture and a restored Victorian kitchen. Adventure woodland and nature trails.
Selkirk. *Halliwell's House.* Large collection of ironmongery, also local history and temporary exhibitions.
Smailholm, nr Kelso. *Smailhom Tower.* 17m high peel tower, built in 15th century as a fortified farmhouse and later used as a border watchtower.
Walkerburn, nr Innerleithen. *Scottish Museum of Wool Textiles.*

CENTRAL (Map pages 54 and 57)

Blair Drummond, nr Doune. *Blair Drummond Leisure and Safari Park.* See page 54.
Bo'ness. *Birkhill Clay Mine.* Tour through the tunnels includes fossilised trees, millions of years old, and the story of fireclay.
Bo'ness. *Hamilton's Cottage.* Recreates a working man's home life in the 1920s. Display of the growth of the town.
Dollar, nr Alloa. *Castle Campbell.* The 15th century stronghold of the Campbell Clan, traditionally known as 'Castle Gloom'. Parapet walk with excellent views.
Doune. *Doune Castle.* 14th century courtyard castle with 4-storey keep, domestic quarters and Lord's Hall.
Doune. *Doune Motor Museum.* Cars from 1905-1984.
Falkirk. *Scottish Railway Preservation Society.* See page 57.
Loch Katrine. *S.S. Sir Walter Scott.* Trips on this old steamer start from east end of loch.
Loch Venacher. *Invertrossachs Nature Reserve.* On south side of loch. Nature trail.
Stirling. *Bannockburn Heritage Centre.*

Exhibition tells you the story of the battle of Bannockburn, where the Scots defeated the English in 1314.
Stirling. *Stirling Castle.* See page 54.

DUMFRIES AND GALLOWAY (Map pages 52 and 55)

Castle Douglas. *Threave Castle.* See page 55. Also *Threave Gardens.*
Clatteringshaws Loch, nr New Galloway. *Clatteringshaws Wildlife Centre.* Displays on local forest wildlife. Also observation of otters, pine martins, wild red deer and wild goats.
Creetown, nr Gatehouse of Fleet. *Cairnholy Chambered Cairns.* See page 55.
Creetown, nr Gatehouse of Fleet. *Gem/Rock Museum.* Rocks, minerals and semi-precious stones from all over the world.
Dumfries. *Burns Heritage Trail.*
Dumfries. *Burns' House.* Home of poet Robert Burns from 1793 to 1796.
Dumfries. *Dumfries Museum.* In a restored 18th century windmill. Has natural history, archaeology and folk collections, and a camera obscura.
Kirkcudbright. *Maclellan's Castle.* A ruined 16th century mansion, overlooking the harbour.
New Abbey, nr Dumfries. *Sweetheart Abbey.* See page 5.
Port Logan, nr Portpatrick. *Logan Botanic Gardens.* Walled and woodland gardens include cabbage palms, tree ferns and a water-garden.
Shearington, nr Dumfries. *Caerlaverock Castle.* Triangular-shaped castle with round towers and moat. Also, *Caerlaverock Wildfowl and Wetlands Trust,* noted for wintering wildfowl.
Thornhill. *Drumlanrig Castle.* Built in 17th century in pink sandstone. Contains furniture and paintings. Adventure woodland and nature trail in parklands.
Wanlockhead, nr Sanquhar. *Museum of the Scottish Lead Mining Industry.* Lead mine tour with mineral collection, beam engine, smelt and miners' cottages. Also hands-on devices.
Wigtown. *Torhouse Stone Circle.* Probably dates from the Bronze Age.

FIFE (Map page 57)

Anstruther. *North Carr Lightship.* Now a floating museum with interior fitted out to show what life was like on board.
Anstruther. *Scottish Fisheries Museum.* Illustrates a Scottish fisherman's life. Includes a marine aquarium.
Arncroach, nr Anstruther. *Kellie Castle and Gardens.* 16th century with plasterwork, painted panelling and Victorian walled garden.
Ceres, nr Cupar. *Fife Folk Museum.* See page 56.
Dunfermline. *Pittencrieff Park.* Has flower gardens, a glen, nature trails, an aviary, old steam-engine, pets' corner and a model traffic area. Also *Pittencrieff House Museum,* with exhibits of local history and costumes.
Falkland. *Falkland Palace.* See page 57.
Lochty, nr Crail. *Lochty Private Railway.* 2½km long steam train rides.
Tentsmuir Point. *Tentsmuir Point National Nature Reserve.* Migrant birds. Nature trail.

GRAMPIAN (Map page 56)

Aberdeen. *James Dun's House.* A museum for children in house of former master of Aberdeen Grammar School.
Aberdeen. *Provost Skene's House.* 17th century furnished house with displays of local history and domestic life.
Alford. *Alford Valley Railway and Museum.*
Ballater. *Balmoral Castle.* One of the homes of the Queen. Grounds sometimes open when Royal Family not in residence.
Ballindalloch, nr Dufftown, *Glenfarclas Distillery.* See page 61.
Banchory. *Crathes Castle and Gardens.* 16th century baronial castle with painted ceilings and famous walled garden. Also adventure playground and nature trail.
Braemar. *Braemar Castle.* Turreted 17th century stronghold, built in an L-shape with a star-shaped curtain wall. Underground pit prison.
Dufftown. *Balvenie Castle.* 13th century moated

castle.
Dufftown. *Glenfiddich and Balvenie Distilleries.* Demonstrations of how malt whisky is made.
Elgin. *Elgin Museum.* Includes fossils, prehistoric weapons, costumes and local domestic items.
Glen Tannar, nr Aboyne. *Braeloine Visitor Centre.* Nature trails and an exhibition about wildlife, farming and forestry in the area.
Kildrummy, nr Alford. *Kildrummy Castle.* Scotland's most complete 13th century castle - known as the 'Queen of Highland Castles'. Headquarters for organising the 1715 Jacobite rising.
Kirkhill of Kennethmont, nr Huntly. *Leith Hall.* Contains military relics. Gardens have pond walk with an observation hide.
Muir of Fowlis, nr Alford. *Craigievar Castle.* See page 56.
Peterculter, nr Aberdeen. *Drum Castle.* 13th century keep adjoining 17th century mansion. Grounds include a garden of historic roses and an adventure playground.
Peterhead. *Arbuthnot Museum.* Local history, whaling and an Arctic section.
Tarland, nr. Ballater. *Culsh Earthworks.* See page 61.

HIGHLAND (Map pages 54, 58-59 and 60-61)

Alltnacaillich, nr Tongue. *Dun Dornadilla Broch.*
Ballachulish. *Glencoe and North Lorn Folk Museum.* Historic relics, domestic and farm implements, weapons, costumes and dolls.
Boat of Garten, nr Aviemore. *Strathspey Railway.* Steam train rides and museum.
Cannich, nr Inverness. *Corrimony Cairn.* Stone Age burial cairn with chamber.
Carrbridge, nr Grantown-on-Spey. *Landmark Visitor Centre.* Includes Highlander show, tree-top trail, nature centre, adventure playground, woodland maze, steam-powered sawmill, giant viewing tower.
Cawdor, nr Nairn. *Cawdor Castle.* See page 60.
Drumnadrochit. *Loch Ness Monster Centre.*
Dunbeath. *Laidhay Caithness Croft.* Croft with stable, house, byre and barn, furnished as it was in 18th century.
Dunvegan, Skye. *Dunvegan Castle.* See page 58. Boat trips from the castle to a seal colony.
Dunvegan, Skye. *Luib Folk Museum.* See page 58.
Durness. *Balnakeil Craft Village.* A wide variety of craftworkers including patchworking, pottery, etc.
Durness. *Smoo Cave.* 3 caves in limestone cliffs. You can take a boat trip inside and see a waterfall.
Fort William. *West Highland Museum.* Displays concerning local history and Bonnie Prince Charlie. Also a re-creation of part of Fort William.
Golspie, nr Dornoch. *Dunrobin Castle.* See page 60.
Handa Island. *Handa Island Nature Reserve.* A seabird sanctuary. Access by boat from Tarbet.
Inverness. *Clava Cairns.* A group of 3 prehistoric burial cairns and standing stones.
Inverness. *Culloden Moor.* Site of battle of Culloden, with clan graves, museum and visitors' centre. See page 60.
Kincraig, nr Aviemore. *Highland Wildlife Park.* See page 31.
Kingussie. *Highland Folk Museum.* See page 61.
Kinlochewe. *Beinn Eighe National Nature Reserve.* Of geological and wildlife interest, with pine marten, wildcat, golden eagle, arctic and alpine plants. Nature trails and visitors' centre.
Knockan, nr Ullapool. *Inverpolly National Nature Reserve.* Nature/geological trail and information centre.
Loch Garten, nr Aviemore. *Loch Garten Nature Reserve.* Ospreys and other wildlife.
Nairn. *Fishertown Museum.* Shows life of Nairn as prosperous fishing town in Victorian times.
Nairn. *Fort George.* See page 60. Also *Queen's Own Highlander's Museum* with medals and uniforms.
Reay, nr Thurso. *Dounreay Nuclear Power Establishment.* Exhibition about work being done at the establishment.
Torridon. *Torridon Visitor Centre.* Nature trails and displays on wildlife. Nearby is *Torridon Deer*

Museum.
Ullapool. *Lochbroom Museum.* History and natural life of region.
Wick. *Wick Heritage Centre.* Exhibition of domestic, fishing and farming life in the area.

LOTHIAN (Map page 57)

East Linton, nr Dunbar. *Preston Mill.* A working water-mill.
Edinburgh. *Craigmillar Castle.* Ruins of huge fortress associated with Mary Queen of Scots.
Edinburgh. *Edinburgh Castle.* Built on a crag. Has great hall, armour, dungeons, state apartments, chapel, Scottish Crown Jewels and Scottish National War Memorial.
Edinburgh. *Museum of Childhood.* Large collection of toys, books, dolls, dolls' houses, costumes and nursery equipment.
Edinburgh. *Royal Museum of Scotland.* Collections show history and everyday life of Scotland from Stone Age to modern times.
Edinburgh. *Camera Obscura and Outlook Tower.*
Edinburgh. *Palace of Holyroodhouse.* See page 57.
Edinburgh. *Philatelic Bureau.* Stamps and historic relics of postal services.
Edinburgh. *Royal Botanic Gardens.* See page 57.
Edinburgh. *The Royal Observatory.*
Edinburgh. *Scottish National Portrait Gallery.*
Edinburgh. *Scottish National Gallery of Modern Art.*
Edinburgh. *Edinburgh Zoo.* See page 30.
Edinburgh. *The Georgian House.* At No.7 Charlotte Square. Rooms furnished as they would have been in the late 1700s.
Linlithgow. *Canal Museum.* History and wildlife of the Union Canal. Barge trips.
Linlithgow. *Linlithgow Palace.* Birthplace of Mary Queen of Scots and home of all the Stewart kings. Now roofless.
Linlithgow. *The House of the Binns.* 17th century house with fine plaster ceilings, panoramic viewpoint and visitor trail.
North Berwick. Boat trips round Bass Rock. See page 57.
North Berwick. *Museum of Flight.* Aircraft, aero-engines and rockets, including Blue Streak.
North Berwick. *Myreton Motor Museum.* Cars, commercial vehicles, motorcycles, bicycles, historic military vehicles and memorabilia.
Prestonpans. *Prestongrange Mining Museum and Historic Site.* On the site of an old colliery. Exhibits include an old beam pumping engine.
South Queensferry. *Hopetoun House.* See page 57.
Stenton, nr Dunbar. *Pressmennan Forest Trail.*
Torphichen, nr Bathgate. *Cairnpapple Hill.* Prehistoric stone circle and burial cairns.

ORKNEY ISLANDS (Map page 63)

Dounby, Mainland. *Click Mill.* A working water-mill.
Finstown, Mainland. *Maes Howe.* Prehistoric chambered tomb with long, stone-lined passage. 12th century runic inscriptions tell of buried treasure.
Kirkwall, Mainland. *Earl Patrick's Palace.* Begun in 1600. Nearby is *Bishop's Palace,* which dates from 1140 and has a 16th century round tower.
Kirkwall, Mainland. *Tankerness House.* An Orkney town house, begun in the 16th century, with courtyard and gardens. Now a museum of life in Orkney over past 5,000 years.
St Mary's, Mainland. *Italian Chapel.* Built by Italian prisoners in World War II out of 2 Nissan huts and scrap metal.
Skaill, nr Stromness, Mainland. *Skara Brae.* A Stone Age village buried under sand dunes until excavation in 1850. You can see stone furniture and hearths, also a museum of artefacts.
Stromness, Mainland. *Standing Stones of Stenness.* Remains of prehistoric stone circle.
Stromness, Mainland. *Stromness Museum.* Preserved birds, eggs and shells, and a maritime section including ship models.
Wyre, Isle of. *Cobbie Row's Castle.* Probably Scotland's oldest stone castle.

SHETLAND ISLANDS (Map page 63)

Lerwick, Mainland. *Shetland Museum.* Life in the Shetlands from prehistoric times to present-day.
Sandwick, Mainland. *Mousa Broch.* Well-preserved Iron Age broch on an island off the mainland.
Sumburgh Head, Mainland. *Jarlshof.* See page 63.
Veensgarth, nr Lerwick, Mainland. *Tingwall Valley Agricultural Museum.* Tools and equipment used by Shetland crofters.

STRATHCLYDE (Map pages 54-55 and 59)

Auchindrain, nr Inverary. *Auchindrain Museum.* Furnished houses and barns showing life on a West Highland farm in 1800s.
Biggar. *Gladstone Court Museum.* See page 52.
Brodick, Arran. *Brodick Castle and Gardens.* See page 55.
Carsaig, Mull. *Carsaig Arches.* Tunnels made by the sea. Reached only at low tide by a 5km walk.
Craignure, Mull. *Duart Castle.* See page 59.
Craignure, Mull. *Torosay Castle.* Victorian house in Scottish baronial style. Italian gardens.
Dervaig, Mull. *Old Byre Folk Museum.* Reconstructions of Mull through the ages by miniature models, videos and slide shows. Also natural history displays.
Dunoon. *Loch Eck,* where rare Powan fish dating back from the Ice Age are found.
Glasgow. *Botanic Gardens.* Includes the Kibble Palace, a 19th century iron glasshouse with tree ferns and Victorian marble statues. Orchids, economic plant section, Palm House, herb garden and arboretum.
Glasgow. *Burrell Collection.* In Pollok Park.
Glasgow. *Haggs Castle Children's Museum.* See page 54.
Glasgow. *Museum of Transport.* See page 55.
Glasgow. *Pollok House.* Adam house with paintings, glass, furniture and pottery. Rhododendrons, woodlands and walks.
Glasgow. *Victoria Park and Fossil Grove.* Includes a flower garden, arboretum and fossil tree-stumps which are 230 million years old.
Glasgow. *The Waverley.* The world's last sea-going paddle steamer. You can cruise in it on the Firth of Clyde during the summer.
Inchcailloch Island, Loch Lomond. *Loch Lomond National Nature Reserve.* Woodland and birds. Access by boat from Balmaha.
Inverary. *Inverary Castle.* See page 54.
Kilmartin, nr Lochgilphead. *Nether Largie Cairns.* Two Bronze Age and one Stone Age burial cairns.
Loch Scridain, Mull. *The Burg.* A fossil tree. Reached by 8km walk on north shore of loch only at low tide.
Maybole. *Culzean Country Park.* Includes an aviary, swan pond and orangery. Also *Culzean Castle.* See page 55.
Millport Island. *University Marine Biological Station. Marine Life Museum* displaying work of the station. Also an aquarium and touch tanks containing shore crabs.
Rothesay, Bute. *Rothesay Castle.* Medieval circular castle with curtain wall.
Staffa, off Mull. *Fingal's Cave.* Huge cave with weird basalt rock formations. Seen by boat trips from Oban or Mull.
Uddingston, nr Glasgow. *Bothwell Castle.* Remains of 13th century stone castle.

TAYSIDE (Map pages 54 and 56-57)

Aberfeldy. *Castle Menzies.* 16th century fortified tower house with turrets, built in the shape of the letter Z.
Arbroath. *St Vigean's Museum.* A cottage museum with gravestones from time of the Picts.
Ben Lawers, nr Loch Tay. *Ben Lawers Visitors' Centre.* Tells the story of the mountain. There is also a nature trail.
Blair Atholl, nr Pitlochry. *Blair Castle.* See page 56.
Braco, nr Crieff. *Ardoch Roman Camp.* Remains of a Roman fort.
Comrie. *Museum of Scottish Tartans.* See page 54.

Dundee. *Broughty Castle Museum.* 4 galleries within the castle include exhibits on whaling, local history, the local seashore and the castle history.
Dundee. *Camperdown Park Wildlife Centre.* Animals and birds, wildlife ponds, woodland nature trails and an information centre.
Dundee. *Mills Observatory.* An astronomical observatory with telescopes you can use and a small planetarium. Also an exhibition on astronomy and space science.
Glamis, nr Forfar. *Angus Folk Museum.* Six 19th century cottages, housing domestic, agricultural and folk collections.
Glamis, nr Forfar. *Glamis Castle.* Historic castle, redesigned in 17th century in style of a French château. Has collections of china, tapestries and furniture and grounds by Capability Brown. See also page 56.
Kinross. *Loch Leven Castle.* On an island in the loch. Access by ferry.
Kinross. *Vane Farm Nature Reserve.* On south shore of Loch Leven. Many wild geese and ducks in winter. Observation centre and nature trail.
Perth. *Scone Palace.* Crowning place of the Scottish kings on the Stone of Destiny. Largely rebuilt in 1803, contains furniture, china, ivories, clocks, vases and needlework. Woodland gardens.
Pitlochry. *Pitlochry Power Station and Dam.* There is an exhibition about hydro-electric power in the power station and you can see salmon in a fish ladder.

WESTERN ISLES (Map pages 58-59)

Arnol, Lewis. *Black House.* A traditional type of house in the Western Isles, furnished and with a byre inside.
Callanish, Lewis. *Callanish Standing Stones.* See page 58.
Carloway, Lewis. *Dun Carloway Broch.* Remains of an Iron Age broch.
Loch Druidibeg, South Uist. *Loch Druidibeg National Nature Reserve.* See page 59.
Shawbost, Lewis. *Shawbost Folk Museum.* There is a restored Scandinavian water-mill nearby.

NORTHERN IRELAND

CO. ANTRIM (Map pages 62-63)

Antrim. *Antrim Castle Park.* 17th century gardens.
Antrim. *The Round Tower.* Remains of a monastery, built in the 6th century.
Antrim. *Shanes Castle.* See page 63.
Ballintoy. *Carrick-a-Rede Rope Bridge.* A narrow bridge made of planks with wire handrails, 24m above the sea to an offshore island.
Belfast. *City of Belfast Zoo.*
Belfast. *Ulster Museum Botanic Gardens.* Displays on the landscape and natural history of Northern Ireland. Also visit the Palm House.
Benvarden, nr Coleraine. *Causeway Safari Park.* Includes lions. Also has a children's zoo, miniature railway and farmyard.
Bushmills. *The Giant's Causeway.* See page 62.
Carrickfergus. *Carrickfergus Castle.* See page 63.
Portrush. *The White Rocks.* Chalk cliffs between Portrush and Dunluce Castle, full of interesting caves and rock formations. Also *Portrush Countryside Centre.* Rock-pool animals in touch tanks.
Rathlin Island. *The Kebble National Nature Reserve.* Reached by motorboat from Ballycastle. A good place for birdwatching.
Whitehead. *Railway Preservation Society of Ireland.* Runs various steam train rides.

CO. ARMAGH (Map page 62)

Armagh. *The Planetarium.* See page 62.
Armagh. *The County Museum.*
Armagh. *Navan Fort.* See page 62.
Portadown. *Ardress House.* 17th century house with plasterwork and pictures. There is a farm museum and wooded grounds.
Portadown. *The Argory.* Neoclassical mansion with stable yard and sundial garden. Some of the rooms are lit by its own gas plant.

CO. DOWN (Map page 63)

Annalong. *Annalong Corn Mill.* Built 1830 and powered by a water-wheel. You can see how flour is made. Water-mills and water-power exhibition.
Ballylesson. *The Giant's Ring.* Huge Stone Age earthwork, with 'The Druid's Altar' dolmen in the middle.
Bangor. *Ward Park.* Includes ponds with waterfowl, nature trail and children's zoo.
Downpatrick. *Ballynoe Stone Circle.*
Greencastle, Carlingford Lough. *Greencastle.* Ruins of a large 13th century Norman fortress.
Holywood, nr Belfast. *Ulster Folk and Transport Museum.* See page 63.
Killyleagh, Strangford Lough. *Killyleagh Castle.* Built in the 12th century, but much altered.
Millisle, nr Donaghadee. *Ballycopeland Windmill.* See page 63. Nearby at Killaughey is a blacksmith's forge.
Newcastle. *Dundrum Castle.* Ruins of a large Norman castle.
Newtownards. *Mount Stewart.* House designed by Robert Adam. Garden includes rare plants and shrubs, topiary and a statuary with figures of dodos, dinosaurs, griffins, etc.
Saintfield. *Rowallane Gardens.*
Strangford. *Castle Ward.* See page 63.
Warrenpoint. *Narrow Water Castle.* 16th century, 3-storey tower, built to defend the estuary.

CO. FERMANAGH (Map page 62)

Belleek. *Belleek Pottery.* See page 62.
Belleek. *Castle Caldwell.* Nature reserve and a ruined castle.
Devenish Island, Lower Lough Erne. *Devenish Round Tower.* 12th century round tower and the remains of a monastery. You can reach the island by ferry.
Enniskillen. *Castlecoole.* 18th century mansion. Contains furnishings and paintings.
Enniskillen. *Enniskillen Castle.*
Enniskillen. *Florence Court.* 18th century house containing fine plasterwork and furniture.
Lisnaskea. *Castle Balfour.* 17th century castle.
Monea. *Monea Castle.* Ruined castle.

CO. LONDONDERRY (Map page 62)

Downhill-Magilligan Point. *Magilligan Strand.* Ireland's longest beach, with lots of different kinds of shells.
Drumsurn. *Kings Fort.* Prehistoric rath (mound) with a deep moat.
Limavady. *Roe Valley Country Park.* Riverside walks with interesting wildlife. Also Ulster's first hydro-electric power station and some old water-mills.
Londonderry. *Londonderry City Walls.* Built in the 17th century, these are the only unbroken walls around any British city.
Moneymore. *Springhill House.* 17th century house with an interesting library and collection of curios, a costume museum and a kitchen.

CO. TYRONE (Map page 62)

Augher. *Knockmany Forest and Chambered Cairn.* The forest is in the Sperrin Mountains, and includes an interesting prehistoric cairn.
Caledon. *Caledon Castle.* Georgian house with interior plasterwork by Adam, and fine paintings. Deer park.
Camphill, nr Omagh. *Ulster American Folk Park.* See page 62.
Cookstown. *Beaghmore Stone Circle.*
Dungannon. *Tyrone Crystal.* You can take a tour round the glass factory.
Kildress, nr Cookstown. *Wellbrook Beetling Mill.* 18th century water-powered mill, with great wheel and sluices in working order.
Newtownstewart. *Baronscourt Forest and Deer Centre.* Includes wildlife and nature exhibition and a nature trail.
Newtownstewart. *Killeter Forest.* Riverside nature trail and red deer.
Omagh. *Seskinore Forest.* Walks, wildlife and many different birds.
Strabane. *Grey's Printing Shop.* An 18th century shop which contains old printing presses.

Map Index

General Index

Useful Addresses

The national or regional tourist boards listed below will be able to give you the addresses of the many local tourist information offices throughout Britain.

National tourist boards

English Tourist Board, Thames Tower, Blacks Rd, Hammersmith, London W6 9EL. Tel: (081) 846 9000
Wales Tourist Board, Brunel House, 2 Fitzalan Place, Cardiff CF2 1UY. Tel: (0222) 499 909
Wales Tourist Board, 12 Regent St, Piccadilly Circus, London SW1Y 4PQ. (Written enquiries only.)
Scottish Tourist Board, 19 Cockspur St, London SW1Y 5BL. Tel: (071) 930 8661
Northern Ireland Tourist Board, St Anne's Court, 59 North St, Belfast BT1 1NB. Tel: (0232) 231 221

Regional Tourist Boards

IN ENGLAND

Cumbria Tourist Board, Ashleigh, Holly Road, Windermere, Cumbria, LA23 2AQ . Tel: (05394) 44444
East Anglia Tourist Board, (counties: Cambs., Essex, Norfolk and Suffolk) Toppersfield Hall, Hadleigh, Suffolk IP7 5DN. Tel: (0473) 822 922
East Midlands Tourist Board, (counties: Derbys., Leics., Lincs., Northants., Notts.), Exchequergate, Lincoln, LN2 1PZ. Tel: (0522) 531 521
Heart of England Tourist Board, (counties: Glos., Heref. and Worc., Shropshire, Staffs., Warks., and W. Midlands), Larkhill Rd, Worcester, WR5 2EF. Tel: (0905) 763 436
London Tourist Board, 26 Grosvenor Gardens, Victoria, London SW1W 0DU. Tel: (071) 730 3450
North West Tourist Board, (counties: Cheshire, Derbys. (High Peak only), Grtr Manchester, Lancs. and Merseyside), Swan House, Swan Meadow Rd, Wigan Pier, Wigan, Lancs. WN3 5BB. Tel: (0942) 821 222
Northumbria Tourist Board, (counties: Cleveland, Durham, Northumberland, Tyne and Wear), Aykley Heads, Durham DH1 5UX. Tel: (091) 384 6905
South East England Tourist Board, (counties: E. Sussex, Kent, Surrey and W. Sussex), The Old Brew House, Warwick Park, Tunbridge Wells, Kent TN2 5TU. Tel: (0892) 540 766
Southern Tourist Board, (counties: parts of Dorset, Hants, Isle of Wight) 40 Chamberlayne Rd, Eastleigh, Hants SO5 5JH. Tel: (0703) 620 006
Thames & Chilterns Tourist Board, (counties: Beds., Berks., Bucks., Herts., Oxfordshire), The Mount House, Church Green, Witney, Oxfordshire OX8 6DZ. Tel: (0993) 778 800

West Country Tourist Board, (counties: Avon, Cornwall, Devon, parts of Dorset, Somerset, Wilts, and Scilly Isles), 60 St David's Hill, Exeter EX4 4SY. Tel: (0392) 76351
Yorkshire & Humberside Tourist Board, (counties: Humberside, N., S. and W. Yorks.), 312 Tadcaster Rd, York YO2 2HF. Tel: (0904) 701 414

IN WALES

Mid Wales Tourism Council, (counties: parts of Dyfed, Gwynned and Powys), The Owain Glyndwr Centre, Machynlleth Powys. Tel: (0654) 702 653
North Wales Tourism, 77 Conway Rd, Colwyn Bay, Clwyd LL29 7LN. Tel: (0492) 531 731
Tourism South Wales, Pemroke House, Charter Court, Phoenix Way, Enterprise Park, Swansea SA7 9DB. Tel: (0792) 781 212

IN SCOTLAND

Aberdeen Tourist Board, St Nicholas House, Broad St, Aberdeen AB9 1DE. Tel: (0224) 632 727
Ayrshire Tourist Board, 39 Sandgate, Ayre. Tel: (0292) 284 196
Scottish Borders Tourist Board, 70 High St, Selkirk TD7 4DD. Tel: (0750) 20555
Dumfries and Galloway Tourist Board, Campbell House, Bankend Rd, Dumfries DG1 4TH. Tel: (0387) 50434
Dundee Tourist Information Centre, 4 City Square, Dundee DD1 3BA. Tel: (0382) 27723
Edinburgh Tourist Information, c/o Edinburgh Marketing Ltd, 3 Princes St, Edinburgh EH2 2QP. Tel: (031) 557 1700
Greater Glasgow Tourist Board, 35-39 St Vincent Place, Glasgow G1 2ER. Tel: (041) 204 4400
Loch Lomond, Stirling and Trossachs Tourist Information Board, 41 Dumbarton Rd, Stirling FK8 2QQ. Tel: 0786 70945
Orkney Tourist Information, 6 Broad St, Kirkwall, Orkney. Tel: (0856) 872 856
St Andrews Tourist Information Office, 78 South St, St Andrews, Fife KY16 9JX. Tel: (0334) 72021
Shetland Islands Tourism, Market Cross, Lerwick, Shetland ZE1 0CU. Tel: (0595) 3434
Western Isles Tourist Organization, 4 South Beach St, Stornoway, Isle of Lewes, PA87 2XY. Tel: (0851) 703 088

Some other organizations mentioned in this book

Countryside Commission, John Dower House, Crescent Place, Cheltenham, Glos. GI50 3RA.
Countryside Commission for Scotland, Battleby, Redgorton, Perth PH1 3EW.
Brecon Beacons National Park, The National Park Office, 7 Glamorgan St, Brecon LD3 7DP.
Dartmoor National Park, Parke, Haytor Rd, Bovey Tracey, Devon TQ13 9JQ.
Exmoor National Park Dept., Exmoor House, Dulverton, Somerset TA22 9HL.
Lake District National Park, National Park Visitor Centre, Brockhole, Windermere, Cumbria LA23 1LJ.
North York Moors National Park, The Old Vicarage, Bondgate, Helmsley, N. Yorks YO6 5BP.
Northumberland National Park, Eastburn, South Park, Hexham, Northumberland NE46 1BS
Peak District National Park, Aldern House, Baslow Rd, Bakewell, Derbys. DE4 1AE.
Pembrokeshire Coast National Park, County Offices, St Thomas' Green, Haverfordwest, Dyfed SA61 1QZ.
Snowdonia National Park, Penrhyndeudraeth, Gwynedd, N. Wales LL48 6LS.
Yorkshire Dales National Park, Colvend, Hebden Rd, Grassington, Skipton, N. Yorks BD23 5LB.
Forestry Commission, 231 Corstorphine Rd, Edinburgh EH12 7AT.
Department of Agriculture (Northern Ireland), Dundonald House, Upper Newtonards Rd, Belfast BT4 3SB.
Department of the Environment (Northern Ireland), Countryside & Wildlife Branch, Calvert House, 23 Castle Place, Belfast BT1 1FY.
National Trust, 36 Queen Anne's Gate, London SW1H 9AS.
National Trust for Scotland, 5 Charlotte Square, Edinburgh EH2 4DU.
National Trust for Northern Ireland, Rowallane House, Saintfield, Ballynahinch, Co. Down BT24 7LH.
Nature Conservancy Council, 19-21 Belgrave Square, London SW1X 8PY
Countryside Council for Wales, Plas Penrhos, Penrhos Rd, Bangor, Gwynedd LL57 2LQ.
Scottish Natural Heritage, 12 Hope Terrace, Edinburgh EH9 2AS.
The Wildfowl & Wetlands Trust, Slimbridge, Glos. GL2 7BT.
Watch, (Wildlife and Environment Club for Young People), The Green, Witham Park, Waterside South, Lincoln LN5 7JR.
World Wide Fund for Nature U.K., Panda House, Weyside Park, Godalming, Surrey GY7 1XR.
British Trust for Conservation Volunteers, 36 St Mary's St, Wallingford, Oxon. OX10 0EU.
Field Studies Council, Preston, Montford, Shrewsbury, Shropshire SY41 HW.
Young Ornithologists' Club, R.S.P.B., The Lodge, Sandy, Beds. SG19 2DL.
British Trust for Ornithology, Beech Grove, Tring, Herts.